McGraw-Hill Education

500
Business
Environment
and Concepts
Questions

for the CPA Exam

McGraw-Hill Education

500
Business
Environment
and Concepts
Questions

for the CPA Exam

Denise M. Stefano, CPA, CGMA, MBA, and Darrel Surett, CPA

New York Chicago San Francisco Athens London Madrid
Mexico City Milan New Delhi Singapore Sydney Toronto

1 2 3 4 5 6 7 8 9 10   QFR/QFR   1 0 9 8 7 6 5 4

ISBN   978-0-07-178984-4
MHID   0-07-178984-7

e-ISBN   978-0-07-178985-1
e-MHID   0-07-178985-5

Library of Congress Control Number 2013957246
Interior artwork by MPS Limited

McGraw-Hill Education products are available at special quantity discounts to use as premiums and sales promotions or for use in corporate training programs. To contact a representative, please visit the Contact Us pages at www.mhprofessional.com.

This book is printed on acid-free paper.

CONTENTS

INTRODUCTION

Congratulations! You've taken a big step toward CPA Exam success by purchasing *McGraw-Hill Education: 500 Business Environment and Concepts Questions for the CPA Exam.* This book gives you 500 multiple-choice questions that cover all the most essential material for the Business Environment and Concepts section of the CPA Exam. Each question is clearly explained in the answer key. The questions will give you valuable independent practice to supplement your other studies.

You might be the kind of student who needs to study extra a few weeks before the exam for a final review. Or you might be the kind of student who puts off preparing until the last minute before the exam. No matter what your preparation style, you will benefit from reviewing these 500 questions, which closely parallel the content, format, and degree of difficulty of the questions on the actual CPA Exam. These questions and the explanations in the answer key are the ideal last-minute study tool for those final weeks before the test.

If you practice with all the questions and answers in this book, we are certain you will build the skills and confidence needed to excel on the CPA Exam. Good luck!

—Editors of McGraw-Hill Education

McGraw-Hill Education

500

Business Environment and Concepts Questions

for the CPA Exam

CHAPTER 1

Operations Management

1. Which of the following performance measures is/are nonfinancial?
   I. Gross margin
   II. Number of days missed due to workplace accidents

   (A) I only
   (B) II only
   (C) Both I and II
   (D) Neither I nor II

2. Measures of nonfinancial performance include
   I. total productivity ratios
   II. partial productivity ratios

   (A) I only
   (B) II only
   (C) Both I and II
   (D) Neither I nor II

3. Which of the following measures of nonfinancial performance would be considered internal benchmarks?
   I. Control charts
   II. Total productivity ratios

   (A) I only
   (B) II only
   (C) Both I and II
   (D) Neither I nor II

4. Which of the following measures of nonfinancial performance would be considered internal benchmarks?
   I. Fishbone diagrams
   II. Pareto diagrams
   (A) I only
   (B) II only
   (C) Both I and II
   (D) Neither I nor II

5. Which of the following nonfinancial measures would monitor the performance of a particular process in relation to acceptable upper and lower limits of deviation?
   I. Control chart
   II. Fishbone diagram
   (A) I only
   (B) II only
   (C) Both I and II
   (D) Neither I nor II

6. An international theme park is having problems with amusement rides that are temporarily closed during peak operations. Quality control wants to begin by repairing the ride that has had the most shutdowns over the previous two months, fix that specific ride, and then move on to the ride with the next most frequent shutdowns. Which diagram or chart would likely be used to determine which ride needs attention first?
   (A) Control chart
   (B) Pareto diagram
   (C) Fishbone diagram
   (D) All of the above

7. Honest John Inc. is a large retailing chain that attempts to offer the lowest possible price on consumer goods. What is the marketing practice that best describes Honest John's approach?
   (A) Interaction-based relationship marketing
   (B) Network marketing
   (C) Transaction marketing
   (D) Database marketing

8. Wickatunk Bike Shop is a retailer that believes that sales advance relationships, thereby driving more sales. Wickatunk Bike Shop is practicing
   I. database marketing
   II. interaction-based relationship marketing
   III. transaction marketing
   (A) II and III
   (B) I only
   (C) I, II, and III
   (D) II only

9. Competitive commission plans tend to emphasize which type of performance compensation?
   I. Future compensation
   II. Current compensation
   (A) I only
   (B) II only
   (C) Both I and II
   (D) Neither I nor II

10. Inventoriable costs include
    I. product costs
    II. period costs
    (A) I only
    (B) II only
    (C) Both I and II
    (D) Neither I nor II

11. Inventoriable costs include which of the following?
    I. Direct materials
    II. Indirect materials
    (A) I only
    (B) II only
    (C) Both I and II
    (D) Neither I nor II

12. Cost drivers
   I. are activities that cause costs to increase as the activity increases
   II. can be financial as well as nonfinancial
   (A) I only
   (B) II only
   (C) Both I and II
   (D) Neither I nor II

13. Falk Manufacturing is attempting to calculate total overhead applied. For the current year, budgeted direct labor hours were 20,000 hours. In addition, budgeted factory overhead was $75,000. Actual costs and hours for the year were as follows:

Direct labor hours	$18,000
Direct labor costs	$103,000
Machine hours	$30,000

   For a particular job, 1,200 direct labor hours were used. Using direct labor hours as the cost driver, what amount of overhead should be applied to this job?
   (A) $5,190
   (B) $4,500
   (C) $5,730
   (D) $6,500

14. In developing a predetermined factory overhead application rate for use in a process costing system, which of the following could be used in the numerator?
   I. Actual factory overhead
   II. Estimated factory overhead
   (A) I only
   (B) II only
   (C) Both I and II
   (D) Neither I nor II

15. In developing a predetermined factory overhead application rate for use in a process costing system, which of the following would generally be used in the denominator?
   I. Actual machine hours
   II. Estimated machine hours
   (A) I only
   (B) II only
   (C) Both I and II
   (D) Neither I nor II

Use the following facts to answer **Questions 16–17**.

Anita Corporation has two major categories of factory overhead: indirect labor and replacement parts for factory machinery. The costs expected for these categories for the coming year are as follows:

Indirect labor	$90,000
Replacement parts for factory machinery	$70,000

Anita currently applies overhead based on direct labor hours. The estimated direct labor hours are 40,000 per year. The plant manager is asked to submit a bid for a potential job and assembles the following data:

Direct materials	$4,000
Direct labor (2,000 hours)	$16,000

16. Which amount reflects the prime costs for the job?

    (A) $4,000
    (B) $16,000
    (C) $20,000
    (D) $28,000

17. What is the total estimated product cost on the proposed job?

    (A) $28,000
    (B) $32,000
    (C) $24,000
    (D) $20,000

18. In the relevant range, fixed costs are

    (A) constant in total but decrease per unit as production levels increase
    (B) constant in total but increase per unit as production levels increase
    (C) constant in total but decrease per unit as production levels decrease
    (D) constant per unit but increase in total as production levels increase

19. Variable costs
    I. per unit remain unchanged in the relevant range
    II. increase in total as unit volume increases

    (A) I only
    (B) II only
    (C) Both I and II
    (D) Neither I nor II

Use the following facts to answer **Questions 20–25**.

Hercules Corporation had the following inventories at the beginning and end of March:

	3/1	3/31
Finished goods	$120,000	$110,000
Work in process	$230,000	$250,000
Direct materials	$134,000	$124,000

The following additional manufacturing data were available for March:

Direct materials purchased	$190,000
Purchase returns and allowances	$1,000
Transportation in	$2,000

Direct labor was $200,000, and factory overhead is applied at a rate of 40 percent of direct labor cost. Actual factory overhead was $165,000.

20. How much direct materials were used during March?

 (A) $325,000
 (B) $223,000
 (C) $199,000
 (D) $201,000

21. What were Hercules' total prime costs for March?

 (A) $200,000
 (B) $400,000
 (C) $401,000
 (D) $435,000

22. How much did Hercules incur in total manufacturing costs for March?

 (A) $566,000
 (B) $525,000
 (C) $711,000
 (D) $481,000

23. Total manufacturing costs available in March were

 (A) $566,000
 (B) $525,000
 (C) $711,000
 (D) $481,000

24. How much was Hercules' cost of goods manufactured for March?
- (A) $481,000
- (B) $461,000
- (C) $501,000
- (D) $485,000

25. How much was Hercules' cost of goods sold for March?
- (A) $451,000
- (B) $461,000
- (C) $471,000
- (D) $481,000

26. For a manufacturing entity, cost of goods sold is equal to cost of goods manufactured
- (A) plus beginning finished goods minus ending finished goods
- (B) plus ending finished goods minus beginning finished goods
- (C) plus beginning finished goods minus ending work in process
- (D) plus ending work in process minus beginning finished goods

27. The cost of goods manufactured differs from the total manufacturing costs in that the cost of goods manufactured
- (A) adds beginning work in process and subtracts ending finished goods
- (B) adds beginning work in process and subtracts beginning finished goods
- (C) adds ending work in process and subtracts beginning work in process
- (D) adds beginning work in process and subtracts ending work in process

28. Ending finished goods inventory is subtracted and beginning finished goods inventory added when attempting to calculate
- (A) cost of goods manufactured
- (B) total manufacturing costs
- (C) overhead applied
- (D) cost of goods sold

29. Micki Corporation uses a job-order cost system and applies manufacturing overhead to jobs using a predetermined overhead rate based on direct labor dollars. The rate for the current year is 200 percent of direct labor dollars. This rate was calculated last November and will be used throughout the current year. During September, direct labor added to jobs was as follows:

	Job #1	Job #2	Job #3
Direct labor	$1,000	$4,500	$2,000

Actual manufacturing overhead for the month of September was $17,500. For September, manufacturing overhead was

(A) overapplied by $2,500
(B) underapplied by $2,500
(C) correctly applied
(D) underapplied by $1,000

30. In a job costing system, issuing indirect materials to production increases which account(s)?
   I. Factory overhead applied
   II. Factory overhead control
(A) I only
(B) II only
(C) Both I and II
(D) Neither I nor II

31. When doing process costing using the weighted average method, what is the first step in determining equivalent units?
(A) Determining ending inventory units
(B) Determining what percentage of the ending inventory units are complete
(C) Determining costs per unit started but not completed
(D) Determining units completed during the period

Use the following facts to answer **Questions 32–37**.

Andrews Manufacturing uses a process costing system to manufacture homogeneous products. The following information summarizes operations during the quarter ending March 31:

Work in process, January 1	100 units
Started during the quarter	500 units
Completed during the quarter	400 units
Work-in-process inventory, March 31	200 units

32. Beginning work-in-process inventory was 50 percent complete for direct materials. Ending work-in-process inventory was 75 percent complete for direct materials. If the actual costs were $650,000 for the current period and $32,000 for the beginning inventory, calculate the equivalent units to be included in the cost per equivalent unit calculation using the weighted average method, with regard to materials for the quarter ended March 31.

    (A) 400 units
    (B) 500 units
    (C) 550 units
    (D) 600 units

33. Beginning work-in-process inventory was 50 percent complete for direct materials. Ending work-in-process inventory was 75 percent complete for direct materials. If the actual costs were $650,000 for the current period and $32,000 for the beginning inventory, how much cost needs to be included in the cost per equivalent unit calculation using the weighted average method, with regard to materials for the quarter ended March 31?

    (A) $32,000
    (B) $682,000
    (C) $650,000
    (D) $511,500

34. Beginning work-in-process inventory was 50 percent complete for direct materials. Ending work-in-process inventory was 75 percent complete for direct materials. If the actual costs were $650,000 for the current period and $32,000 for the beginning inventory, what is the cost per equivalent unit of production using the weighted average method, with regard to materials for the quarter ended March 31?

    (A) $1,240
    (B) $1,182
    (C) $1,300
    (D) $1,364

35. Beginning work-in-process inventory was 50 percent complete for direct materials. Ending work-in-process inventory was 75 percent complete for direct materials. If the actual costs were $650,000 for the current period and $32,000 for the beginning inventory, calculate the equivalent units to be included in the cost per equivalent unit calculation using the FIFO method, with regard to materials for the quarter ended March 31.

   (A) 400 units
   (B) 500 units
   (C) 550 units
   (D) 600 units

36. Beginning work-in-process inventory was 50 percent complete for direct materials. Ending work-in-process inventory was 75 percent complete for direct materials. If the actual costs were $650,000 for the current period and $32,000 for the beginning inventory, how much cost needs to be included in the calculation of cost per equivalent unit using the FIFO method, with regard to materials for the quarter ended March 31?

   (A) $32,000
   (B) $682,000
   (C) $650,000
   (D) $511,500

37. Beginning work-in-process inventory was 50 percent complete for direct materials. Ending work-in-process inventory was 75 percent complete for direct materials. If the actual costs were $650,000 for the current period and $32,000 for the beginning inventory, calculate the cost per equivalent unit of production using the FIFO method, with regard to materials for the quarter ended March 31.

   (A) $1,240
   (B) $1,300
   (C) $1,083
   (D) $1,364

38. In process costing, which of the following would be included in total costs when calculating cost per equivalent unit under the weighted average assumption?
   I. Costs of units completed during the period
   II. Costs of beginning inventory

   (A) I only
   (B) II only
   (C) Both I and II
   (D) Neither I nor II

39. In process costing, when determining cost per equivalent unit, the number of equivalent units in the denominator will include *beginning inventory units* if the cost flow assumption being used is
   I. weighted average
   II. FIFO

   (A) I only
   (B) II only
   (C) Both I and II
   (D) Neither I nor II

40. In process costing, which of the following would be included in the numerator when calculating cost per equivalent unit under the FIFO assumption?
   I. Current costs
   II. Beginning inventory costs

   (A) I only
   (B) II only
   (C) Both I and II
   (D) Neither I nor II

41. Under process costing, which of the following cost flow assumptions would include ending inventory times the percentage of completion in the calculation for the number of equivalent units?
   I. Weighted average
   II. FIFO

   (A) I only
   (B) II only
   (C) Both I and II
   (D) Neither I nor II

42. Under process costing, when determining cost per unit, which of the following methods would consider beginning inventory units but NOT beginning inventory costs?
   I. Weighted average
   II. FIFO

   (A) I only
   (B) II only
   (C) Both I and II
   (D) Neither I nor II

43. Which of the following describes a system that accumulates all costs of overhead for each of the departments or activities of the organization and then allocates those overhead costs based on causal factors?

(A) Process costing
(B) Job-order costing
(C) Activity-based costing
(D) None of the above

44. What benefits can management expect from activity-based costing?

   I. It provides management with a more thorough understanding of product costs and product profitability for strategies and pricing decisions.
   II. It leads to a more competitive position by evaluating cost drivers.
   III. It uses a common departmental or factory-wide measure of activity, such as direct labor hours or dollars, to distribute manufacturing overhead to products.

(A) I and II
(B) I and III
(C) II and III
(D) I, II, and III

45. Eliminating all cost drivers would eliminate which of the following?

   I. Value-adding activities
   II. Nonvalue-adding activities

(A) I only
(B) II only
(C) Both I and II
(D) Neither I nor II

46. Which of the following can be used to allocate production costs to products and services by averaging the cost over the total units produced?

   I. Job-order costing
   II. Process costing
   III. Activity-based costing

(A) I only
(B) I and II
(C) II and III
(D) II only

47. Activity-based costing includes
    I. using cost drivers as application bases to increase the accuracy of reported product costs
    II. using several machine cost pools to measure product costs on the basis of time in a machine center
    III. using application rates that are plant-wide rather than incurring the cost of detailed allocations

    (A) I and III
    (B) I and II
    (C) II only
    (D) I, II, and III

48. Which of the following would be an appropriate costing method for internal but NOT external reporting?
    I. Activity-based costing
    II. Job-order costing
    III. Process costing

    (A) I only
    (B) II and III
    (C) I, II, and III
    (D) None of the above

49. Tammy Manufacturing uses direct costing. At the end of its first year of operations, 2,000 units of inventory are on hand. Fixed manufacturing costs are $40 per unit. Which of the following statements is/are correct?
    I. The use of absorption costing, rather than variable costing, would result in a higher net income.
    II. The use of absorption costing, rather than variable costing, would result in a higher ending inventory.

    (A) I only
    (B) II only
    (C) Both I and II
    (D) Neither I nor II

50. Which of the following could be used to refer to the contribution approach?
    I. Direct costing
    II. Full absorption costing
    III. Variable costing

    (A) III only
    (B) I and III
    (C) I only
    (D) I, II, and III

51. Direct costing can be used for financial reporting that is
    I. internal
    II. external

    (A) I only
    (B) II only
    (C) Both I and II
    (D) Neither I nor II

52. Under absorption costing, costs are broken down between which of the following?
    I. Fixed and variable
    II. Product and period

    (A) I only
    (B) II only
    (C) Both I and II
    (D) Neither I nor II

53. Under variable costing,
    I. all fixed factory overhead is treated as a period cost and is expensed in the period incurred
    II. cost of goods sold includes only variable costs

    (A) I only
    (B) II only
    (C) Both I and II
    (D) Neither I nor II

54. Under variable costing, which of the following would be expensed in the period incurred?

    I. Fixed selling, general, and administrative expenses

   II. Fixed factory overhead

(A) I only

(B) II only

(C) Both I and II

(D) Neither I nor II

55. Which of the following would appear in ending inventory under absorption costing but NOT under direct costing?

(A) Fixed selling and administrative costs

(B) Variable selling and administrative costs

(C) Fixed manufacturing costs

(D) Variable manufacturing costs

Use the following facts to answer **Questions 56–58**.

In Year 1, its first year of operation, Pecorino Manufacturers had the following manufacturing costs when it produced 100,000 and sold 75,000 units of its only product:

Fixed costs	$195,000
Variable costs	$160,000

56. Under direct costing, how much fixed manufacturing cost will be expensed in Year 1?

(A) $0

(B) $48,750

(C) $146,250

(D) $195,000

57. Under full absorption costing, how much fixed manufacturing cost will be expensed in Year 1?

(A) $0

(B) $48,750

(C) $146,250

(D) $195,000

58. What is the difference in net income between absorption costing and direct costing?

(A) $0
(B) $48,750
(C) $146,250
(D) $195,000

59. Which of the following is/are correct regarding the relationship between direct costing and full absorption costing as it relates to production and sales?

   I. When production exceeds sales, net income under absorption costing is higher than net income under direct costing.

   II. When sales exceed production, absorption costing net income is less than variable costing net income.

(A) I only
(B) II only
(C) Both I and II
(D) Neither I nor II

60. Selected information concerning Owen Industries Inc. for the year ended December 31 is as follows:

Units produced	40,000
Units sold	37,000
Direct materials used	$180,000
Direct labor incurred	$140,000
Fixed factory overhead	$150,000
Variable factory overhead	$124,000
Fixed selling and administrative expenses	$160,000
Variable selling and administrative expenses	$19,000

    Work-in-process inventories at the beginning and end of the year were zero. What was Owen Industries' finished goods inventory cost at December 31 under the direct (variable) costing method?

(A) $33,300
(B) $44,550
(C) $47,250
(D) $49,360

61. Under the contribution approach, which of the following would contain only variable costs?
   I. Ending inventory
  II. Cost of goods sold

(A) I only
(B) II only
(C) Both I and II
(D) Neither I nor II

62. Under direct costing, which of the following is subtracted from sales to calculate contribution margin?

(A) All variable costs
(B) Variable overhead but not variable selling expenses
(C) Variable selling expenses but not variable overhead
(D) Variable overhead and fixed overhead

63. Under direct costing, variable overhead is included in the calculation of which of the following?
   I. Contribution margin
  II. Cost of goods sold

(A) I only
(B) II only
(C) Both I and II
(D) Neither I nor II

64. Under the contribution approach, variable selling and general expenses are included in the calculation of which of the following?
   I. Contribution margin
  II. Cost of goods sold

(A) I only
(B) II only
(C) Both I and II
(D) Neither I nor II

65. Under direct costing, when calculating contribution margin,

(A) variable manufacturing costs are included as well as fixed manufacturing costs
(B) variable manufacturing costs are included as well as variable selling and general expenses
(C) variable selling and general expenses are included as well as fixed selling and general expenses
(D) variable manufacturing costs are included but not variable selling and general expenses

66. The following information pertains to Tatum Corporation:

Sales	$750,000
Manufacturing costs	$210,000 (fixed), $140,000 (variable)
Selling and administrative costs	$300,000 (fixed), $45,000 (variable)

　　If Tatum produces and sells 30,000 units, how much is the contribution margin?

(A) $565,000
(B) $410,000
(C) $355,000
(D) $265,000

Use the following facts to answer **Questions 67–68**.

Ridge Corporation is a manufacturer. One of its products, "chip," is used as a spare part for military and civilian vehicles. This product has the following financial structure per unit in Year 1:

Selling price	$160
Direct materials	$20
Direct labor	$15
Variable manufacturing overhead	$12
Fixed manufacturing overhead	$30
Shipping and handling—freight out	$3
Fixed selling and administrative costs	$10
Total costs	$90

67. How much is the contribution margin for one unit of product "chip"?

(A) $110
(B) $113
(C) $120
(D) $150

68. If total sales are 18,000 units and sales returns are $80,000, what is the total contribution margin for Year 1?

(A) $2,000,000
(B) $1,980,000
(C) $1,900,000
(D) $900,000

69. Barry Inc. is a manufacturer. Which of the following would increase for Barry if production and sales were to increase?
    I. Variable costs per unit
   II. Contribution margin per unit

(A) I only
(B) II only
(C) Both I and II
(D) Neither I nor II

70. The following information relates to Griffin Corporation, which produced and sold 55,000 units during Year 1:

Sales	$750,000
Fixed manufacturing costs	$310,000
Variable manufacturing costs	$130,000
Fixed selling and administrative costs	$200,000
Variable selling and administrative costs	$45,000

    For Year 2, if production and sales are expected to be 60,000 units, Griffin should anticipate a contribution margin per unit of

(A) $10.45
(B) $11.73
(C) $12.09
(D) $13.29

71. Homer Company developed its business plan based on the assumption that units would sell at a price of $400 each. The variable costs for each unit were projected at $200, and the annual fixed costs were budgeted at $80,000. Homer's after-tax profit objective was $160,000; the company's effective tax rate is 30 percent. If no changes are made to the selling price or cost structure, determine the number of units that Homer must sell in order to break even.

(A) 400
(B) 367
(C) 350
(D) 250

72. Island Ridge Manufacturing has variable costs of 20 percent of sales and fixed costs of $30,000. What is Island Ridge's breakeven point in sales dollars?

(A) $60,500
(B) $30,500
(C) $24,500
(D) $37,500

Use the following facts to answer **Questions 73–76**.

In Year 1, Scully Manufacturing sells products for $7.50 each. Variable costs of manufacturing are $2.25 per unit.

73. The company needs to sell 20,000 units to break even. How much are fixed costs?
    (A) $45,000
    (B) $105,000
    (C) $150,000
    (D) Need more information to solve

74. In Year 2, Scully Manufacturing expects the units to sell for $9. Variable manufacturing costs are expected to increase by one-third, and fixed costs are expected to increase by 20 percent. How much is the new contribution margin per unit for Year 2?
    (A) $9
    (B) $6.75
    (C) $6
    (D) $4.50

75. In Year 2, Scully Manufacturing expects the units to sell for $9. Variable manufacturing costs are expected to increase by one-third, and fixed costs are expected to increase by 20 percent. How much does Scully expect total fixed costs to be in Year 2?
    (A) $105,000
    (B) $115,500
    (C) $125,000
    (D) $126,000

76. In Year 2, Scully Manufacturing expects the units to sell for $9. Variable manufacturing costs are expected to increase by one-third, and fixed costs are expected to increase by 20 percent. How many units does Scully need to sell to break even in Year 2?
    (A) 20,750
    (B) 20,000
    (C) 21,000
    (D) 22,000

Use the following facts to answer **Questions 77–79**.

Franco Company manufactures helmets with direct material costs of $10 per unit and direct labor of $7 per unit. A regional freight company charges Franco $5 per unit to make deliveries. Sales commissions are paid at 10 percent of the selling price. Helmets are sold for $100 each. Indirect factory costs and administrative costs are $5,000 and $20,200 per month, respectively.

77. How much are total variable costs per unit?
    (A) $17
    (B) $22
    (C) $32
    (D) $37

78. How much are Franco's fixed costs?
    (A) $5,000
    (B) $20,200
    (C) $25,200
    (D) None of the above

79. How many helmets must Franco produce to break even?
    (A) 371
    (B) 421
    (C) 547
    (D) 631

80. Musk Corporation developed its business plan based on the assumption that products would sell at a price of $400 each. The variable costs for each product were projected at $200, and the annual fixed costs were budgeted at $100,000. Musk's profit objective was $240,000. If no changes are made to the selling price or cost structure, determine the number of units that Musk must sell to achieve its profit objective.
    (A) 4,500
    (B) 3,500
    (C) 1,700
    (D) 2,500

81. Gold Manufacturing makes mini solar panels and has the following cost structure:

Direct materials	$3.25
Direct labor	$4
Freight out	$0.75
Total fixed costs	$100,000

How many panels must Gold Manufacturing sell to earn a profit of $50,000 before taxes if the selling price is $20 per unit?

(A) 8,333
(B) 12,500
(C) 14,166
(D) 15,000

82. Harbor Manufacturing earned a profit in Year 1 of $95,000 before tax. The tax rate for Year 1 was 30 percent. In Year 2, Harbor desires an after-tax profit of $100,000, and the tax rate for Year 2 is 35 percent. How much pretax profit does Harbor need to earn to reach its desired after-tax profit goal?

(A) $122,564
(B) $153,846
(C) $150,000
(D) $164,346

Use the following facts to answer **Questions 83–84**.

Spotswood Corporation is a manufacturer with the following information for Year 1:

Sales	$200,000
Contribution margin	$120,000
Fixed costs	$70,000
Income taxes	$10,000

83. How much is breakeven in dollars?

(A) $90,000
(B) $124,444
(C) $81,665
(D) $116,667

84. How much is the margin of safety?

(A) $50,000
(B) $70,000
(C) $82,667
(D) $83,333

85. Breakeven analysis assumes that over the relevant range which of the following will occur?

I. Variable cost per unit will change with volume.
II. Fixed cost will remain constant.

(A) I only
(B) II only
(C) Both I and II
(D) Neither I nor II

86. Breakeven analysis assumes that which of the following would be constant on a per unit basis?

I. All variable costs
II. Revenue

(A) I only
(B) II only
(C) Both I and II
(D) Neither I nor II

87. When considering a special order, a manufacturer would accept the order if the sales price were in excess of which of the following?

(A) Variable costs
(B) Opportunity costs
(C) Relevant costs
(D) Fixed costs

88. At full capacity, relevant costs of accepting a special order include which of the following?

I. Contribution margin in dollars that will be forfeited to produce the special order
II. Variable costs

(A) I only
(B) II only
(C) Both I and II
(D) Neither I nor II

89. Mosca Company has considerable excess manufacturing capacity. A special job order's cost sheet includes the following applied manufacturing overhead costs:

Fixed costs $11,000
Variable costs $23,000

    The fixed costs include a normal $2,700 allocation for in-house design costs, although no in-house design will be done. Instead the job will require the use of external designers costing $8,750. What is the total amount to be included in the calculation to determine the minimum acceptable price for the job?

(A) $31,750
(B) $34,000
(C) $37,050
(D) $44,000

90. Which of the following assumptions underlie(s) cost-volume-profit analysis?
    I. Total variable costs are directly proportional to volume over a relevant range.
    II. Selling prices are to remain unchanged.

(A) I only
(B) II only
(C) Both I and II
(D) Neither I nor II

91. Norcross Corporation is offered a one-time special order for its product and has the capacity to take this order without losing current business. Variable costs per unit and fixed costs in total will be the same. The gross profit for the special order will be 20 percent, which is 10 percent less than the usual gross profit. What impact will this order have on total fixed costs and operating income?

(A) Total fixed costs increase, and operating income increases.
(B) Total fixed costs do not change, and operating income increases.
(C) Total fixed costs decrease, and fixed costs per unit increase.
(D) Total fixed costs do not change, and operating income does not change.

92. What is the term for the potential benefit lost by selecting a particular course of action?

(A) Contribution margin
(B) Variable cost per unit
(C) Opportunity cost
(D) Breakeven point in units

93. When deciding on whether to accept a special order, if idle space has no alternative use, which of the following would be correct?
    I. Opportunity cost would be zero.
    II. The special order would be accepted if the selling price was more than the variable cost per unit.
    (A) I only
    (B) II only
    (C) Both I and II
    (D) Neither I nor II

94. Whether to make or purchase a product is NOT influenced by fixed costs that are
    I. avoidable
    II. unavoidable
    (A) I only
    (B) II only
    (C) Both I and II
    (D) Neither I nor II

95. Howard Corporation has a factory with idle space and is deciding whether to build more units or rent out the space. Opportunity cost is equal to the
    (A) combined value of the opportunity selected and the next best use
    (B) difference between the best alternative and the next best alternative
    (C) most profitable use of the factory space
    (D) value of the next best alternative

96. Tillman Corporation had an opportunity to use its capacity to produce an extra 4,000 units with a contribution margin of $5 per unit or to rent out the space for $15,000. What was the opportunity cost of using the capacity?
    (A) $20,000
    (B) $5,000
    (C) $15,000
    (D) $35,000

97. The relevance of a particular cost to a decision is determined by which of the following?
    I. Potential effect on the decision of the particular cost
    II. The number of decision alternatives
    (A) I only
    (B) II only
    (C) Both I and II
    (D) Neither I nor II

98. Fascination Corporation is a clothing manufacturer. In a decision analysis situation, which of the following costs would be relevant to a decision?
   I. Avoidable cost
   II. Incremental cost

(A) I only
(B) II only
(C) Both I and II
(D) Neither I nor II

99. The operational decision method, referred to as marginal analysis, is used when analyzing business decisions such as which of the following?
   I. The introduction of a new product
   II. Whether to change output levels of existing products

(A) I only
(B) II only
(C) Both I and II
(D) Neither I nor II

100. The operational decision method, referred to as marginal analysis, would NOT be useful when analyzing which of the following business decisions?
   I. Accepting or rejecting special orders
   II. Making versus buying a product or service

(A) I only
(B) II only
(C) Both I and II
(D) Neither I nor II

101. When considering alternatives, such as make or buy, costs that will change under different alternatives
   I. are known as relevant costs
   II. should be considered by management unless they vary with production

(A) I only
(B) II only
(C) Both I and II
(D) Neither I nor II

102. Which of the following costs would NOT be considered in a decision to sell or process further?

    I. Joint costs

   II. Separable costs

(A) I only

(B) II only

(C) Both I and II

(D) Neither I nor II

Use the following facts to answer **Questions 103–104.**

Hathaway Corporation manufactures two products from a joint process. The two products developed are product "Quo" and product "Rael." A standard production run incurs joint costs of $150,000 and results in 30,000 units of Quo and 60,000 units of Rael. Each Quo sells for $3 per unit; each Rael sells for $6 per unit.

103. Assuming no further processing work is done after the split-off point, how much joint cost should be allocated to product Rael based on total quantity of units produced?

(A) $50,000

(B) $100,000

(C) $150,000

(D) None of the above

104. Each Quo sells for $3 per unit; each Rael sells for $6 per unit. If there are no further processing costs incurred after the split-off point, how much joint cost should be allocated to Rael using the relative sales value method?

(A) $30,000

(B) $60,000

(C) $90,000

(D) $120,000

105. Manning Corporation produced two products, product A and product B. A standard production run resulted in joint cost of $400,000. At the split-off point, Manning anticipates 30,000 units of product A and 20,000 units of product B. If Manning sold all of the products at the split-off point, product A would sell for $5.50 and product B for $7. If there are no further processing costs incurred after the split-off point, how much of the joint cost should Manning allocate to product A on a physical quantity allocation basis?

(A) $200,000

(B) $300,000

(C) $240,000

(D) $350,000

106. In a decision analysis situation, relevant costs include
   I. incremental costs
   II. prime costs

   (A) I only
   (B) II only
   (C) Both I and II
   (D) Neither I nor II

107. Fanny Manufacturing is deciding whether to keep or drop a segment of its business. Which costs and benefits are compared in reaching that decision?

   (A) The cost of contribution margin lost is compared to unavoidable fixed costs.
   (B) Avoidable fixed costs are compared to the profit or loss from the segment.
   (C) Profit or loss from the segment is compared to profit or loss for the entire company.
   (D) The cost of contribution margin lost is compared to avoidable fixed costs.

108. A regression equation is based on an estimate of the _____ based on changes in the _____.

   (A) independent variable, dependent variable
   (B) dependent variable, independent variable
   (C) dependent variable, dependent variable
   (D) independent variable, independent variable

109. Which of the following measures the strength of the relationship between the dependent variable and the independent variable in a number between −1.0 and 1.0?

   (A) Total cost
   (B) Correlation coefficient
   (C) Learning curve
   (D) Linear regression equation

Use the following facts to answer **Questions 110–113**.

Assume the regression analysis results for Rayon Manufacturing Corporation can be shown as: $y = 80x + 25$.

110. What does y represent?
    (A) Fixed costs
    (B) Total costs
    (C) Variable costs
    (D) The independent variable

111. What does the 25 represent?
    (A) Fixed costs
    (B) Total costs
    (C) Variable costs
    (D) The independent variable

112. If the budget calls for producing 150 units, which of the following could be a correlation coefficient for the relationship between volume and total cost?
    (A) 0.85
    (B) −0.79
    (C) 0
    (D) 2.0

113. If the budget calls for producing 150 units, and the coefficient of variation is 85 percent, which of the following would be correct?
    I. Total cost is equal to $12,000.
    II. The coefficient of determination measures the proportion of the total variation in "y"—or total cost—that is explained by the total variation in the independent variable, x, or variable costs.
    (A) I only
    (B) II only
    (C) Both I and II
    (D) Neither I nor II

114. Sayre Corporation uses the coefficient of correlation to measure the strength of the cost volume relationships used in planning. Which of the following would be correct regarding costs and volume with respect to the coefficient of correlation?
    I. Cost volume relationships are not only positive but also assumed to be proportional.
    II. A coefficient of correlation of zero would NOT be expected for fixed costs.
    (A) I only
    (B) II only
    (C) Both I and II
    (D) Neither I nor II

115. When selecting cost drivers or independent variables, management would LEAST likely select a cost driver with a correlation coefficient of
    (A) −1.0
    (B) 1.0
    (C) 0.005
    (D) 0.50

116. When forecasting total cost, management would likely select a cost driver or independent variable if the correlation coefficient were which of the following?
    I. Positive
    II. Negative
    III. Zero
    (A) I only
    (B) I and III
    (C) II and III
    (D) I and II

117. Which of the following would NOT be used to classify costs as either fixed or variable?
    I. High-low method
    II. Regression analysis method
    (A) I only
    (B) II only
    (C) Both I and II
    (D) Neither I nor II

Use the following facts to answer **Questions 118–119**.

Meadows Corporation applied the high-low estimation for customer order data from July 1 through December 31 of Year 8.

Period	Volume	Cost
July	420	$7,260
Aug	470	$7,840
Sept	370	$6,935
Oct	364	$6,834
Nov	410	$7,110
Dec	520	$8,350

118. How much was variable cost per order?

(A) $8.80
(B) $9.72
(C) $10.40
(D) $10.88

119. How much was fixed cost for December?

(A) $3,754
(B) $3,296
(C) $2,814
(D) $2,645

CHAPTER 2

Planning and Budgeting

120. Participative budgeting can be characterized by which of the following?
  I. Increased motivation
  II. More time consuming
  III. Decreased acceptance

  (A) I and II
  (B) II and III
  (C) I and III
  (D) I, II, and III

121. Which of the following types of budgets would NOT be contained in the master budget?
  I. Operating budgets
  II. Financial budgets

  (A) I only
  (B) II only
  (C) Both I and II
  (D) Neither I nor II

122. Which of the following would be found in the operating rather than the financial budget?
  I. Pro forma income statement
  II. Capital expenditures budget

  (A) I only
  (B) II only
  (C) Both I and II
  (D) Neither I nor II

123. Which of the following budgets is/are generally produced BEFORE the sales budget?

    I. Production budget

    II. Cash budget

(A) I only

(B) II only

(C) Both I and II

(D) Neither I nor II

124. In the budgeting process, which of the following is/are prepared after the cash budget?

    I. Sales budget

    II. Pro forma financial statements

(A) I only

(B) II only

(C) Both I and II

(D) Neither I nor II

125. Which of the following budgets is prepared independently of the sales budget?

(A) Production budget

(B) Selling and administrative budget

(C) Cash budget

(D) Capital expenditures budget

126. Which of the following budgets are appropriate for planning because they involve both fixed and variable costs?

    I. Flexible budgets

    II. Static budgets

(A) I only

(B) II only

(C) Both I and II

(D) Neither I nor II

127. A static budget

    I. is based on costs at one level of output

    II. includes budgeted costs for actual and budgeted output

(A) I only

(B) II only

(C) Both I and II

(D) Neither I nor II

128. The annual business plan typically begins with operating budgets driven by which of the following?
    (A) Financial budgets
    (B) Production budgets
    (C) Personnel budgets
    (D) Sales budgets

129. Of the four budgets listed, what is the proper order in which they are prepared?
    I. Cash disbursements budget
    II. Production budget
    III. Direct materials budget
    IV. Sales budget
    (A) IV, II, III, I
    (B) IV, I, III, II
    (C) III, II, IV, I
    (D) I, II, III, IV

130. What are sales forecasts based upon?
    I. Past patterns of sales
    II. Changes in the firm's prices
    III. Results of market research studies
    (A) I and II
    (B) I, II, and III
    (C) II and III
    (D) I and III

131. What is the required unit production level given the following factors?

Projected sales	2,000
Beginning inventory	185
Desired ending inventory	220
Prior-year beginning inventory	30

    (A) 1,965 units
    (B) 2,035 units
    (C) 1,995 units
    (D) 1,935 units

132. A company's controller is adjusting next year's budget to reflect the impact of an expected 4 percent inflation rate. Listed are selected items from next year's budget before the adjustment:

Salaries expense	$210,000
Insurance expense	$120,000
Supplies expense	$60,000

After adjusting for the 4 percent inflation rate, what is the company's total budget for the selected items before taxes for next year?

(A) $380,000
(B) $395,800
(C) $401,200
(D) $405,600

133. A company's controller is adjusting next year's budget to reflect the impact of an expected 4 percent inflation rate. Listed are selected items from next year's budget before the adjustment:

Salaries expense	$210,000
Insurance expense	$120,000
Supplies expense	$60,000
Depreciation expense	$25,000
Interest expense on 10-year fixed rate bonds	$27,000

After adjusting for the 4 percent inflation rate, what is the company's total budget for the selected items before taxes for next year?

(A) $459,680
(B) $458,680
(C) $458,350
(D) $457,600

134. Rascal Company plans to produce 100,000 toy fire trucks during July. Planned production for August is 150,000 trucks. Sales are forecasted at 90,000 trucks for July and 110,000 trucks for August. Each truck has eight wheels. Rascal's policy is to maintain 5 percent of the next month's production in inventory at the end of a month. How many wheels should Rascal purchase during July?

(A) 860,000
(B) 820,000
(C) 810,000
(D) 780,000

135. Mallard Inc. is in the process of preparing its annual budget. The following beginning and ending inventory levels (in units) are planned for the year ending December 31, Year 4:

	Beginning Inventory	Ending Inventory
Raw material	30,000	40,000
Work in process	20,000	20,000
Finished goods	60,000	40,000

Two units of raw material are needed to produce each unit of finished product. If Mallard plans to sell 380,000 units during Year 4, how many units would it have to manufacture during the year?

(A) 400,000 units
(B) 360,000 units
(C) 350,000 units
(D) 325,000 units

136. The sales budget for Wagner Industries shows quarterly sales for the next year as follows:

Quarter	Units
1	11,000
2	9,000
3	12,000
4	16,000

Wagner's policy is to have a finished goods inventory at the end of each quarter equal to 10 percent of the next quarter's sales. What would budgeted production for the second quarter of the next year be?

(A) 8,700 units
(B) 9,300 units
(C) 9,550 units
(D) 9,900 units

137. Yanna Corporation manufactures computer tables. The tabletops are manufactured by Yanna, but the keyboard draw is purchased from an outside supplier. The Assembly Department takes a manufactured table and attaches the keyboard draw. It takes 30 minutes of labor to assemble a keyboard draw to a table. The company follows a policy of producing enough tables to ensure that 30 percent of next month's sales are in the finished goods inventory. Yanna also purchases sufficient raw materials to ensure that raw materials inventory is 55 percent of the following month's scheduled production. Yanna's sales budget in units for the fourth quarter of Year 1 follows:

October	2,400
November	3,000
December	2,100

Yanna's ending inventories in units for September 30, Year 1, are:

Finished goods	1,600
Raw materials (keyboard draws)	3,800

What is the number of computer tables to be produced during November in Year 1?

(A) 1,825 tables
(B) 2,210 tables
(C) 2,340 tables
(D) 2,730 tables

138. Tucker Tool and Dye has developed the following production plan:

Month	Units
January	11,000
February	13,000
March	8,000
April	10,000

Each unit contains three pounds of raw material. The desired raw material ending inventory each month is 120 percent of the next month's production, plus 500 pounds. (The beginning inventory meets this requirement.) Tucker has developed the following direct labor standards for production of these units:

	Department 1	Department 2
Hours per unit	3.0	0.5
Hourly rate	$6.75	$10

Tucker's total budgeted direct labor dollars for March usage should be

(A) $162,000
(B) $122,000
(C) $202,000
(D) $192,000

139. Inputs in calculating a cost of goods manufactured budget include which of the following?
  I. Overhead applied
  II. Material usage

(A) I only
(B) II only
(C) Both I and II
(D) Neither I nor II

140. Inputs in calculating a cost of goods manufactured budget include which of the following?
  I. Finished goods inventory
  II. Work-in-process inventory

(A) I only
(B) II only
(C) Both I and II
(D) Neither I nor II

141. The selling and administrative expense budget can be correctly described as
    I. a financial rather than an operational budget
    II. dependent upon sales

    (A) I only
    (B) II only
    (C) Both I and II
    (D) Neither I nor II

142. Stirling Corporation is preparing a Year 1 cash budget for the purchase of merchandise. Budgeted data are:

Cost of goods sold for Year 1	$200,000
Accounts payable, Jan. 1, Year 1	$20,000
Inventory, Jan. 1, Year 1	$30,000
Inventory, Dec. 31, Year 1	$43,000

    Purchases will be made in 12 equal monthly amounts and paid for in the following month. What is Stirling's Year 1 budgeted cash payment for purchases of merchandise?

    (A) $210,750
    (B) $215,250
    (C) $226,250
    (D) $245,000

143. The cash budget shows itemized cash receipts and disbursements during the period, including the
    I. financing activities
    II. beginning cash balances

    (A) I only
    (B) II only
    (C) Both I and II
    (D) Neither I nor II

144. Which of the following is/are correct regarding a cash budget?
    I. The cash budget shows the availability of funds for repayment of debt.
    II. The cash budget is usually NOT broken down into monthly periods.

    (A) I only
    (B) II only
    (C) Both I and II
    (D) Neither I nor II

145. Singer Company budgeted sales on account of $200,000 for October, $250,000 for November, and $275,000 for December. Collection experience indicates that 70 percent of the budgeted sales will be collected the month after the sale, 26 percent the second month, and 4 percent will be uncollectible. The cash receipts from accounts receivable that should be budgeted for December would be

(A) $198,250
(B) $199,700
(C) $147,700
(D) $191,712

146. Levin Inc. is preparing a schedule of cash receipts and disbursements for Year 4. Which of the following items should be included?
  I. Borrowing funds from a bank on a note payable taken out in August Year 4 and agreeing to pay the principal and interest in July Year 5
  II. Dividends declared in October Year 4 to be paid in January Year 5 to shareholders of record as of December Year 4

(A) I only
(B) II only
(C) Both I and II
(D) Neither I nor II

147. Which of the following would NOT be included in a statement of cash receipts and disbursements for KingPin Corporation in Year 2?
  I. A purchase order issued in December Year 2 for items to be delivered in January Year 3
  II. The amount of uncollectible customer accounts for Year 2

(A) I only
(B) II only
(C) Both I and II
(D) Neither I nor II

148. Norris Company forecasted first quarter sales of 10,000 units, second quarter sales of 15,000 units, third quarter sales of 14,000 units, and fourth quarter sales of 17,000 units at $4 per unit. Past experience has shown that 70 percent of the sales will be in cash and 30 percent will be on credit. All credit sales are collected in the following quarter, and none are uncollectible. What amount of cash is forecasted to be collected in the second quarter?

(A) $54,000
(B) $42,000
(C) $30,000
(D) $28,500

149. Which of the following budgeted (pro forma) financial statements is prepared first?

(A) Pro forma statement of cash flows
(B) Pro forma income statement
(C) Pro forma balance sheet
(D) May be prepared in any order

150. Flexible budgeting is limited because it is highly dependent upon an accurate identification of

I. fixed cost
II. variable cost per unit

(A) I only
(B) II only
(C) Both I and II
(D) Neither I nor II

151. Planned additions of capital equipment from the capital budget are added to the

I. pro forma balance sheet
II. cash budget

(A) I only
(B) II only
(C) Both I and II
(D) Neither I nor II

152. A flexible budget would NOT be appropriate for

    I. service industries

    II. a direct labor usage budget

(A) I only

(B) II only

(C) Both I and II

(D) Neither I nor II

153. When calculating net income using flexible budgeting, which of the following would be assumed constant within a relevant range?

    I. Variable cost per unit

    II. Total fixed cost

    III. Selling price per unit

(A) II only

(B) I and II

(C) II and III

(D) I, II, and III

154. A flexible budget contains

(A) budgeted costs for budgeted output

(B) actual costs for budgeted output

(C) budgeted costs for actual output

(D) actual costs for actual output

Use the following facts to answer **Questions 155–156**.

Hyson Inc. manufactures and sells products. The master budget and the actual results for July are as follows:

	Actual July Sales	Master Budget
Unit sales	12,000	10,000
Sales	$132,000	$100,000
Variable costs	$70,800	$60,000
Contribution margin	$61,200	$40,000
Fixed costs	$30,000	$25,000
Operating income	$31,200	$15,000

155. If flexible budgeting is used, how much is contribution margin per unit based on actual sales of 12,000 units?

   (A) $4.00
   (B) $5.10
   (C) $4.55
   (D) None of the above

156. How much is the operating income for Hyson Inc. using a flexible budget for July?

   (A) $31,200
   (B) $21,000
   (C) $23,000
   (D) $15,000

Use the following facts to answer **Questions 157–158**.

Gilbert Watches sells a line of wrist wear. Gilbert's performance report for March Year 4 follows:

	Actual	Static Budget
Watches sold	500	600
Sales	$24,000	$30,000
Variable costs	$14,500	$18,000
Contribution margin	$9,500	$12,000
Fixed costs	$8,100	$8,800

157. If Gilbert Watches uses a flexible budget to analyze its performance, the variable cost flexible budget variance for March is

(A) $500 unfavorable
(B) $500 favorable
(C) $3,500 unfavorable
(D) $3,500 favorable

158. The fixed cost variance for March is

(A) $700 unfavorable
(B) $700 favorable
(C) $2,500 favorable
(D) $300 unfavorable

159. The initial budget forecast for Jayson Corporation was production of 10,000 units during the year with a variable cost of $10 per unit. Jayson produced 9,000 units during the year. Actual variable manufacturing costs were $89,000. What is Jayson's flexible budget variance for the year?

(A) $1,000 unfavorable
(B) $11,000 favorable
(C) $1,000 favorable
(D) $11,000 unfavorable

160. Which of the following would NOT be a purpose for identifying manufacturing variances and assigning their responsibility to a person or department?

    I. To promote learning and improve operations
    II. To provide useful information about pricing of finished goods

    (A) I only
    (B) II only
    (C) Both I and II
    (D) Neither I nor II

161. A company budgeted the need for 10,000 materials at a price of $30 per unit. The actual units needed turned out to be 11,400 at a price of $28.50 per unit. What is the company's materials price variance?

    (A) $15,000 unfavorable
    (B) $17,100 unfavorable
    (C) $17,100 favorable
    (D) $15,000 favorable

162. For the current period production levels, Imhoff Company budgeted 12,300 board feet of production and purchased 15,000 board feet. The material cost was budgeted at $7 per foot. The actual cost for the period was $9.50 per foot. What was Imhoff's material price variance for the period?

    (A) $37,500 favorable
    (B) $30,750 favorable
    (C) $30,750 unfavorable
    (D) $37,500 unfavorable

163. The difference between standard hours at standard wage rates and actual hours at standard rates is referred to as

    (A) indirect labor variance
    (B) direct labor rate variance
    (C) direct labor rate
    (D) direct labor efficiency variance

164. Romeo Manufacturing has relevant information for material Tyrisis as follows:

Quantity purchased	3,500 pounds
Standard quantity allowed	3,000 pounds
Actual price	$4.80
Standard price	$5

What was the direct material price variance for material Tyrisis?

(A) $700 unfavorable
(B) $600 unfavorable
(C) $600 favorable
(D) $700 favorable

165. The direct labor efficiency variance

   I. could be unfavorable as a result of an unfavorable material usage variance
  II. is calculated by using the standard wage rate rather than the actual wage rate

(A) I only
(B) II only
(C) Both I and II
(D) Neither I nor II

166. When analyzing unfavorable variances, inadequate supervision may explain the reason behind an unfavorable

   I. material price variance
  II. labor usage variance

(A) I only
(B) II only
(C) Both I and II
(D) Neither I nor II

167. The purchase of higher than standard quality material would likely result in

(A) an unfavorable material price variance and a favorable material usage variance
(B) a favorable material price variance but an unfavorable material efficiency variance
(C) an unfavorable material price variance and an unfavorable material usage variance
(D) a favorable material usage variance and a favorable material price variance

Use the following facts to answer **Questions 168–169**.

Mojo Inc. manufactures backup generators and uses a standard cost system. The following information is available for the month of September:

80,000 direct labor hours were budgeted.
A total of 84,000 direct labor hours were worked at a total cost of $840,000.
The standard direct labor rate is $9 per hour.
The standard direct labor time per unit is four hours.

168. The direct labor price variance for September was

    (A) $84,000 favorable
    (B) $84,000 unfavorable
    (C) $79,000 unfavorable
    (D) $79,000 favorable

169. Mojo planned on producing 25,000 generators, but only 20,000 were actually produced. What was the direct labor efficiency variance for September?

    (A) $36,000 unfavorable
    (B) $36,000 favorable
    (C) $40,000 unfavorable
    (D) $40,000 favorable

Use the following facts to answer **Questions 170–171**.

Barlow Enterprises uses a standard cost system. The standard cost information regarding materials needed to manufacture one unit is 60 pounds of material at $1.70 per pound. The standard cost for labor needed to manufacture one unit of Tull is three hours at $12 per hour. During October, Barlow produced 1,750 units of Tull compared to a normal capacity of 1,900 units. The actual costs per unit of materials and labor were as follows:

Materials purchased and used	59 pounds at $1.85 per pound
Labor	3.5 hours at $12.50 per hour

170. Barlow's material price variance for October is

    (A) $15,750 unfavorable
    (B) $15,488 favorable
    (C) $15,750 favorable
    (D) $15,488 unfavorable

171. Barlow's labor rate variance for October is

    (A) $875 unfavorable
    (B) $875 favorable
    (C) $3,063 unfavorable
    (D) $3,063 favorable

172. Gabriel Corporation uses a standard costing system. At the end of the current year, the company provides the following overhead information:

Actual direct labor hours	10,000
Actual overhead incurred	$80,000 (variable), $52,000 (fixed)
Budgeted fixed overhead	$55,000
Variable overhead rate (per direct labor hour)	$9
Standard hours allowed for actual production	11,000

What is Gabriel's variable overhead efficiency variance?

(A) 0
(B) $9,000 unfavorable
(C) $9,000 favorable
(D) $19,000 favorable

173. Ryan Corporation budgeted sales of 5,250 at $13 per unit but sold 4,000 at $16 per unit. Ryan would compute a selling price variance of

(A) $3,750 unfavorable
(B) $12,000 favorable
(C) $15,750 favorable
(D) $4,250 favorable

174. Harper Company has gathered the following information from a recent production run:

Standard variable overhead rate	$20
Actual variable overhead rate	$16
Standard process hours	44
Actual process hours	50

What is the company's variable overhead spending variance?

(A) $200 favorable
(B) $200 unfavorable
(C) $176 favorable
(D) $176 unfavorable

175. Which of the following can occur when the quantity budgeted to be sold differs from the quantity actually sold?

   I. Sales price variance
  II. Sales volume variance

(A) I only
(B) II only
(C) Both I and II
(D) Neither I nor II

176. Which of the following can be used to monitor the purchasing manager's performance?

(A) Direct material usage variance
(B) Direct labor rate variance
(C) Indirect material usage variance
(D) Direct material price variance

177. The balanced scorecard integrates which of the following measures of performance?

I. Financial performance
II. Nonfinancial performance

(A) I only
(B) II only
(C) Both I and II
(D) Neither I nor II

178. Which of the following could be used as an example of responsibility accounting?

I. Cost center
II. Profit center
III. Investment center

(A) I and III
(B) II and III
(C) I and II
(D) I, II, and III

179. Strategic business units (SBUs) are classified into different types based on the responsibility levels assigned to their managers. Put the following SBUs in order from least responsibility to greatest responsibility.

I. Profit SBU
II. Cost SBU
III. Revenue SBU
IV. Investment capital SBU

(A) II, IV, I, III
(B) II, I, III, IV
(C) II, III, I, IV
(D) IV, II, I, III

180. The balanced scorecard reports management information regarding organizational performance as defined by "critical success factors." These critical success factors are often classified as

   I. human resources
   II. business process
   III. customer satisfaction
   IV. financial performance

(A) I, III, and IV
(B) I, II, and IV
(C) II, III, and IV
(D) I, II, III, and IV

181. Responsibility accounting defines a "profit center" as being responsible for

   I. revenues
   II. costs
   III. invested capital

(A) I and III
(B) I, II, and III
(C) I only
(D) I and II

182. How does responsibility accounting define and describe an investment center?

   I. An investment center is responsible for revenues, expenses, and invested capital.
   II. An investment center is similar to an independent business.

(A) I only
(B) II only
(C) Both I and II
(D) Neither I nor II

183. Which of the following would be contained in a performance report for a cost center?

   I. Controllable costs
   II. Controllable revenues

(A) I only
(B) II only
(C) Both I and II
(D) Neither I nor II

184. The financial perspective of a balanced scorecard is concerned with which of the following?
   I. Capture of increased market share
  II. Employee satisfaction and retention measures

(A) I only
(B) II only
(C) Both I and II
(D) Neither I nor II

185. The "internal business" perspective of the balanced scorecard measures
   I. results of business operations through improved efficiencies
  II. nonfinancial performance such as employee satisfaction and retention

(A) I only
(B) II only
(C) Both I and II
(D) Neither I nor II

186. Which section of the balanced scorecard would focus on results of operations and utilization of assets?
   I. Customer
  II. Financial
 III. Learning and innovation

(A) II only
(B) I and II
(C) II and III
(D) I, II, and III

187. Sales less variable costs less controllable fixed costs is referred to as the

(A) contribution margin
(B) controllable margin
(C) overhead efficiency variance
(D) volume variance

188. Which of the following is/are correct regarding controllable margin?
   I. Controllable margins are specifically defined as contribution margin less controllable fixed costs.
  II. The reporting objective of controllable margin is to most clearly define those margins for which a manager is responsible.

(A) I only
(B) II only
(C) Both I and II
(D) Neither I nor II

CHAPTER 3

Financial Management

189. In evaluating costs for decision-making, a company would consider which of the following as relevant?
   I. Differential costs
   II. Incremental costs
   III. Avoidable costs

(A) I and III
(B) I, II, and III
(C) II and III
(D) I and II

190. In evaluating costs for decision-making, a company would NOT generally consider which of the following as relevant?
   I. Discretionary costs
   II. Opportunity costs
   III. Sunk costs

(A) I and III
(B) II and III
(C) III only
(D) I, II, and III

191. In a decision analysis situation, which of the following would be relevant costs?
   I. Unavoidable fixed costs
   II. Potential productivity loss due to employee morale
   III. Opportunity costs

(A) I, II, and III
(B) II and III
(C) I and III
(D) III only

Use the following facts to answer **Questions 192–195**.

Battaglia Corporation is considering the acquisition of a new machine. The machine can be purchased for $100,000; it will cost $4,000 to install and $7,000 to transport to Battaglia's plant. It is estimated that the machine will last 10 years, and it is expected to be worth $4,000 after it's fully depreciated. Over its 10-year life, the machine is expected to produce 3,000 units per year with a selling price of $300 and combined material and labor costs of $250 per unit. Federal tax regulations permit machines of this type to be depreciated using the straight-line method over 7 years with no consideration for salvage value. Battaglia has a marginal tax rate of 30 percent.

192. What is the net cash outflow at the beginning of the first year that Battaglia Corporation should use in a capital budgeting analysis?

   (A) $100,000
   (B) $107,000
   (C) $111,000
   (D) $97,500

193. How much depreciation should Battaglia include in the calculation of after-tax cash flow in its capital budgeting analysis for Year 2?

   (A) $15,857
   (B) $13,059
   (C) $11,500
   (D) $11,100

194. What is the net cash flow for the second year that Battaglia should use in a capital budgeting analysis?

   (A) $150,000
   (B) $109,757
   (C) $134,143
   (D) $40,243

195. What is the net cash flow for Year 10 of the project that Battaglia should use in a capital budgeting analysis?

   (A) $105,000
   (B) $107,800
   (C) $109,800
   (D) $109,000

196. Crellin Inc. is considering purchasing a new machine to replace an older, inefficient model. The new machine has a cost of $320,000. The old machine has a value of $9,500. Which of the following costs would NOT be included in a capital budgeting analysis as part of the net cash outflow of the new machine?
 I. Transportation cost of the new machine
 II. Installation cost of the new machine
 III. Depreciation expense times the tax rate

(A) III only
(B) I and III
(C) II and III
(D) None of the above

197. Herbie's Auto Shop purchased an asset for $90,000 that has no salvage value and a 10-year life. Herbie's effective income tax rate is 30 percent, and it uses the straight-line depreciation method for income tax reporting purposes. For book purposes, Herbie will also depreciate this asset using the straight-line method, and there is an expected salvage value of $10,000. Herbie's annual depreciation tax shield from the asset would be

(A) $9,000
(B) $2,700
(C) $6,300
(D) $2,400

198. Most capital budgeting techniques, including net present value, focus on
 I. cash flow
 II. net income
 III. earnings before interest and taxes

(A) I and III
(B) I and II
(C) I only
(D) I, II, and III

199. In equipment replacement decisions, which of the following costs are relevant?
 I. Original fair market value of the old equipment
 II. Current salvage value of the old equipment
 III. Operating costs of the new equipment
 IV. Cost of the new equipment

(A) I, II, III, and IV
(B) II and III
(C) I, III, and IV
(D) II, III, and IV

200. Olney Company owns land that could be developed in the future. Olney estimates it can sell the land to Ritter Inc. for $950,000 net of all selling costs. If the land is not sold, Olney will continue with its plans to build three single-family homes on the land. If Olney decided to develop the property, what type of cost would the potential selling price of the land represent in Olney's decision?

(A) Sunk
(B) Incremental
(C) Opportunity
(D) Variable

Use the following facts to answer **Questions 201–202.**

Aron Company is trying to decide whether to keep an existing machine or replace it with a new machine. The old machine was purchased just 2 years ago for $40,000 and had an expected life of 12 years. It now costs $1,300 a month for maintenance and repairs. A new machine is being considered to replace it at a cost of $50,000. The new machine is more efficient, and it will cost only $120 a month for maintenance and repairs. The new machine has an expected life of 12 years.

201. In deciding to replace the old machine, which of the following is a sunk cost?

(A) $50,000
(B) $1,300 per month
(C) $120 per month
(D) $40,000

202. Which of the following factors would Aron consider when deciding whether to replace the machine?
   I. Any estimated salvage value of the old machine
   II. The lower maintenance cost of the new machine
   III. The estimated salvage value of the new machine

(A) I and II
(B) I, II, and III
(C) II and III
(D) I and III

203. Capell Corporation makes an investment of $250,000 with a useful life of 10 years (no salvage value) and expects to use this investment to generate $370,000 in sales with $290,000 in incremental operating costs. If the company operates in an environment with a 40 percent tax rate, what are the expected after-tax cash flows that Capell will use to evaluate the capital investment decision?

(A) $10,000
(B) $23,000
(C) $48,000
(D) $58,000

Use the following facts to answer **Questions 204–205**.

Cace Corporation is deciding whether to replace an asset. A new asset costing $50,000 can be purchased to replace the existing asset that originally cost the company $40,000 and has accumulated depreciation of $32,000. A vendor of Cace has offered $13,300 for the old asset.

204. Assuming a tax rate of 30 percent, which of the following would be relevant when making the decision whether to replace the old asset?
   I. Purchase price of new asset
  II. Purchase price of old asset
 III. Accumulated depreciation of old asset

(A) I, II, and III
(B) I only
(C) I and III
(D) I and II

205. How much of the gain on the sale of the old asset is relevant to the decision of replacing the old asset?

(A) $1,590
(B) $5,300
(C) $3,710
(D) $13,300

206. When applying cash flows with discounting to business decisions, the calculation of annual net cash inflow
   I. includes the cash inflow times 1 minus the tax rate
  II. includes depreciation expense times 1 minus the tax rate

(A) I only
(B) II only
(C) Both I and II
(D) Neither I nor II

207. Which of the following methods of capital budgeting would require managers to evaluate the dollar amount of return?

(A) Net present value
(B) Internal rate of return
(C) Payback method
(D) All of the above

208. Which of the following would be an advantage of using the net present value method of analyzing capital budgeting decisions?

 I. The net present value method can be used when there is a different rate of return for each year of the project.
 II. The net present value method indicates whether an investment will earn the hurdle rate of return.

(A) I only
(B) II only
(C) Both I and II
(D) Neither I nor II

209. The Truncale Company is planning a $210,000 equipment investment that has an estimated five-year life with no estimated salvage value. The present value of an annuity due for five years is 6.109. The company has projected the following annual cash flows for the investment:

Year	Projected Cash Flows	Present Value of $1
1	$120,000	0.91
2	$60,000	0.76
3	$40,000	0.63
4	$40,000	0.53
5	$40,000	0.44
Total	$300,000	3.27

The net present value for this investment is

(A) ($3,800)
(B) $8,800
(C) $2,548
(D) ($800)

210. If the net present value of a project is positive, it would indicate that
    I. the rate of return for the project is less than the discount percentage rate (hurdle rate) used in the net present value computation
    II. the present value of cash outflows is less than the present value of cash inflows

(A) I only
(B) II only
(C) Both I and II
(D) Neither I nor II

211. Weiskoff Company is considering a project that yields annual net cash inflows of $430,000 for Years 1 through 5, and a net cash inflow of $90,000 in Year 6. The project will require an initial investment of $1,750,000. Weiskoff's cost of capital is 10 percent. Present value information is:

Present value of $1 for five years at 10 percent is 0.65.
Present value of $1 for six years at 10 percent is 0.59.
Present value of an annuity of $1 for five years at 10 percent is 3.83.

    What is Weiskoff's expected net present value for this project?

(A) $5,400
(B) ($50,000)
(C) $53,100
(D) $50,000

212. Dean Inc. is investing in a machine with a three-year life. The machine is expected to reduce annual cash operating costs by $40,000 in each of the first two years and by $30,000 in the third year. Which of the following is/are correct?
    I. To calculate the present value of the savings for Years 1 and 2, the factor for the present value of an annuity of $1 for two periods is used.
    II. To calculate the present value of the savings for Year 3, the factor for the lump sum of a present value of $1 for three periods is required.

(A) I only
(B) II only
(C) Both I and II
(D) Neither I nor II

213. The discount rate where the present value of the inflows is equal to the outflows is known as the

(A) net present value
(B) internal rate of return
(C) profitability index
(D) All of the above

214. Which of the following is/are correct regarding the internal rate of return?

   I. The internal rate of return method determines the present value factor and related interest rate that yields a net present value equal to zero.
   II. The internal rate of return focuses the decision maker on the discount rate at which the present value of the cash inflows equals the initial investment.
   III. Projects with an internal rate of return greater than the hurdle rate should be rejected.

(A) I and III
(B) I and II
(C) I, II, and III
(D) I only

215. Which of the following would be an advantage of the payback method?

   I. It is easy to understand.
   II. It does NOT consider the time value of money.

(A) I only
(B) II only
(C) Both I and II
(D) Neither I nor II

216. In discounted cash flow analysis, which of the following would illustrate a difference between the net present value method and the internal rate of return?

   I. When using the net present value method, different hurdle rates can be used for each year of the project.
   II. The net present value method uses discounted cash flows and the internal rate of return does NOT.

(A) I only
(B) II only
(C) Both I and II
(D) Neither I nor II

217. In evaluating a capital budget project, the use of the net present value model is NOT generally affected by the
    I. project's tax depreciation allowance
    II. amount of added working capital needed for operations during the term of the project

(A) I only
(B) II only
(C) Both I and II
(D) Neither I nor II

218. The discounted cash flow model is considered the best for long-term decisions. Which of the following are discounted cash flow methods?
    I. Net present value
    II. Internal rate of return
    III. Profitability index

(A) I, II, and III
(B) I and II
(C) I and III
(D) II and III

219. The discounted cash flow model is considered the best for long-term decisions. Which of the following is a discounted cash flow method?
    I. Accounting rate of return
    II. Payback method

(A) I only
(B) II only
(C) Both I and II
(D) Neither I nor II

220. If the profitability index of a project is exactly 1.0, which of the following is correct?

(A) The present value of the outflows is greater than the present value of the inflows.
(B) The present value of the inflows is greater than the present value of the outflows.
(C) The present value of the inflows is equal to the present value of the outflows.
(D) None of the above

221. Pry Inc. is evaluating a capital investment proposal for a new machine. The investment proposal shows the following information:

Initial cost	$600,000
Life	4 years
Annual net cash inflows	$220,000
Salvage value	$100,000

If acquired, the machine will be depreciated using the straight-line method. What is the payback period for this investment?

(A) 2.27
(B) 2.73
(C) 2.84
(D) 3.0

222. Which of the following methods of analyzing investment alternatives ignore(s) cash flows after the initial investment has been recovered?
  I. Payback method
 II. Discounted payback method
III. Net present value

(A) II only
(B) I, II, and III
(C) I only
(D) I and II

223. Limitations of the net present value method and the internal rate of return include which of the following?
  I. They rely on the forecasting of future data.
 II. They consider the time value of money.

(A) I only
(B) II only
(C) Both I and II
(D) Neither I nor II

224. Alden Corporation purchases equipment for $46,000. The salvage value of the equipment is $6,000. Pertinent information follows:

Year	Net Cash Flows	Present Value
1	$9,000	0.943
2	$15,000	0.841
3	$19,000	0.776
4	$25,000	0.719

What is the discounted payback period in years?

(A) 3.484 years
(B) 3.217 years
(C) 3.692 years
(D) 3.564 years

225. Which of the following is often calculated using trial and error by dividing the investment by the cash inflows to equal a desired present value factor?

(A) Net present value
(B) Internal rate of return
(C) Payback method
(D) Accounting rate of return

226. Which of the following describe the net present value method?
  I. It assumes that positive cash flows are reinvested at the hurdle rate.
  II. It measures the value of capital investments in dollars and considers the time value of money.
  III. It uses the accrual basis, not the cash basis.

(A) II and III
(B) I and III
(C) I, II, and III
(D) I and II

227. Which of the following methods would NOT be useful for determining total project profitability?
  I. Discounted payback method
  II. Net present value

(A) I only
(B) II only
(C) Both I and II
(D) Neither I nor II

228. The profitability index
  I. is used to rank investments
  II. is calculated by taking the total investment and dividing by annual cash flows
  III. expresses the net present value in terms of a percentage
  (A) I and II
  (B) I, II, and III
  (C) II and III
  (D) I and III

Use the following facts to answer **Questions 229–230**.

Blauser Corporation is considering purchasing a machine that costs $90,000 and has a $15,000 salvage value. The machine will provide net annual cash inflows of $20,000 per year and a net income of $12,000 per year. It has a five-year life. The corporation uses a discount rate of 9 percent. The discount factor for the present value of a single sum five years in the future is 0.618. The discount factor for the present value of an annuity for five years is 3.847.

229. What is the present value of the cash inflows?
  (A) $76,940
  (B) $86,210
  (C) $90,000
  (D) $82,428

230. How much is the net present value of the machine?
  (A) $15,210
  (B) $9,270
  (C) ($22,330)
  (D) ($3,790)

231. Mullin Company is considering the purchase of a new machine that costs $560,000. The new machine will generate net cash flow of $125,000 per year and net income of $90,000 per year for five years. Mullin's desired rate of return is 7 percent. The present value factor for a five-year annuity of $1, discounted at 7 percent, is 4.698. The present value factor of $1, at compound interest of 7 percent due in five years, is 0.789. What is the new machine's net present value?
  (A) $27,250
  (B) ($27,250)
  (C) ($137,180)
  (D) $18,250

232. Dupree Corporation is evaluating its potential investment in a piece of equipment with a four-year life and no salvage value. The tax rate is 35 percent. Discounted pretax cash flows are $399,874, undiscounted after-tax cash flows are $286,600, and discounted after-tax cash flows are $237,992. The company's hurdle rate is 9 percent, and it anticipates that pretax cash flows in each of the three years will equal 25 percent, 30 percent, and 50 percent, respectively, of the investment's face value. If the investment costs $244,500, what is the net present value of the investment?

(A) ($6,508)
(B) $6,508
(C) ($42,100)
(D) None of the above

233. Kendrick Corporation is evaluating an investment in a piece of equipment with a four-year life and no salvage value. The equipment has a cost of $218,340. Kendrick anticipates that pretax cash flows in each of the four years will equal 10 percent, 32 percent, 40 percent, and 30 percent, respectively, of the investment's face value. The tax rate is 30 percent. Pretax cash flows, discounted at 9.5 percent, are $387,655, undiscounted after-tax cash flows are $262,171, and after-tax cash flows, discounted at 9.5 percent, are $218,340. Calculate the internal rate of return.

(A) 9.5 percent
(B) 10 percent
(C) 11.5 percent
(D) Cannot be determined from the information given

234. In this form of capital budgeting, project cash flows are discounted based upon a predetermined discount rate and compared to the investment in the project to arrive at a positive or negative dollar amount.
  I. Net present value
 II. Internal rate of return
III. Accounting rate of return

(A) I and II
(B) I, II, and III
(C) II and III
(D) I only

235. Which of the following is correct regarding operating leverage?

(A) Operating leverage is defined as the degree to which a firm uses fixed operating costs as opposed to variable operating costs.

(B) Operating leverage is defined as the degree to which a firm uses variable operating costs as opposed to fixed operating costs.

(C) Operating leverage results from the use of both fixed operating costs and fixed financing costs to magnify returns to the firm's owners.

(D) Operating leverage is defined as the degree to which a firm uses debt to finance the firm.

236. A firm's degree of operating leverage is calculated by which of the following formulas?

(A) Percent change in sales divided by percent change in earnings before interest and taxes

(B) Percent change in earnings before interest and taxes divided by percent change in sales

(C) Percent change in earnings per share divided by percent change in earnings before interest and taxes

(D) Percent change in earnings before interest and taxes divided by percent change in earnings per share

237. A firm's degree of financial leverage is calculated by which of the following formulas?

(A) Percent change in sales divided by percent change in earnings before interest and taxes

(B) Percent change in earnings before interest and taxes divided by percent change in sales

(C) Percent change in earnings per share divided by percent change in earnings before interest and taxes

(D) Percent change in earnings before interest and taxes divided by percent change in earnings per share

238. When a firm has a relatively high degree of operating leverage,

I. a small increase in sales can lead to a large increase in profit because fixed costs remain the same over a relevant range

II. variable operating costs are high relative to fixed operating costs

(A) I only

(B) II only

(C) Both I and II

(D) Neither I nor II

239. Which of the following can be defined as the degree to which a firm uses debt to finance the firm?
  I. Financial leverage
  II. Operating leverage
  (A) I only
  (B) II only
  (C) Both I and II
  (D) Neither I nor II

240. Vista Company has a degree of operating leverage of 4 after experiencing a 24 percent increase in earnings before interest and taxes as a result of earning additional revenue. What percentage of additional revenue did Vista Company earn in order to experience a 24 percent increase in earnings before interest and taxes?
  (A) 20 percent
  (B) 96 percent
  (C) 4 percent
  (D) 6 percent

241. Company A experiences an increase in sales of 6 percent and an increase in earnings before interest and taxes of 18 percent. Company B experiences an increase in earnings before interest and taxes of 10 percent after a 5 percent increase in sales. Which of the following would be correct?
  I. Company A has a higher degree of operating leverage than company B.
  II. Company A has relatively lower variable operating costs and higher fixed operating costs compared to company B.
  (A) I only
  (B) II only
  (C) Both I and II
  (D) Neither I nor II

242. Which of the following is/are correct regarding operating leverage?
  I. If a firm has high operating leverage, a relatively small decrease in sales will have a potentially greater decrease in shareholder value.
  II. The higher the firm's operating leverage, the higher the potential profit.
  (A) I only
  (B) II only
  (C) Both I and II
  (D) Neither I nor II

243. Combined financial leverage is calculated by

(A) adding total operating leverage plus financial leverage
(B) multiplying operating leverage times financial leverage
(C) dividing the percent change in earnings before interest and taxes by percent change in sales
(D) dividing the percent change in earnings per share by percent change in earnings before interest and taxes

244. Which of the following would be defined as the degree to which a firm uses debt to finance the firm?

   I. Financial leverage
  II. Operating leverage
 III. Combined leverage

(A) I and II
(B) I only
(C) I and III
(D) I, II, and III

245. The capital structure of Royce Corporation includes bonds with a coupon rate of 11 percent and an effective interest rate of 13 percent. The corporate tax rate is 40 percent. What is Royce's net cost of debt?

(A) 6.6 percent
(B) 5.2 percent
(C) 7.1 percent
(D) 7.8 percent

Use the following facts to answer **Questions 246–249.**

Anderson's debt is 30 percent of its capital structure, its preferred stock is 10 percent, and common stock is the remainder. The cost of common stock is 10 percent; preferred stock and debt have a cost of 10 percent each. Anderson's marginal tax rate is 25 percent.

246. How much is Anderson's weighted average cost of debt capital?

(A) 7.5 percent
(B) 2.25 percent
(C) 5.25 percent
(D) 3 percent

247. How much is Anderson's weighted average cost of its preferred stock?

(A) 1.2 percent
(B) Less than 1 percent
(C) More than 2 percent but less than 3 percent
(D) 1 percent

248. How much is Anderson's weighted average cost of common stock?

(A) 6 percent
(B) 10 percent
(C) 7.5 percent
(D) 4.5 percent

249. How much is Anderson's weighted average cost of capital?

(A) 7 percent
(B) 8.25 percent
(C) 9.25 percent
(D) 12 percent

250. The weighted average cost of capital is the average cost of which of the following given a firm's existing assets and operations?

 I. Debt financing
 II. Equity financing

(A) I only
(B) II only
(C) Both I and II
(D) Neither I nor II

251. Which of the following would be correct regarding the optimal capital structure and the weighted average cost of capital (WACC)?

 I. The optimal cost of capital is the ratio of debt to equity that produces the lowest WACC.
 II. If the debt to equity ratio increases, investors will likely demand a greater return.

(A) I only
(B) II only
(C) Both I and II
(D) Neither I nor II

252. Strat-O-Matic is a wholesaler and retailer of board and computer games. Using the capital asset pricing model (CAPM), how much is the required rate of return for Strat-O-Matic assuming a beta of 0.95 when the market return is 12 percent and the risk-free rate is 5 percent?

(A) 7 percent
(B) 13 percent
(C) 11.65 percent
(D) 10.95 percent

253. Valley Corporation is issuing debt to raise capital. Which of the following would be correct regarding the cost of debt capital to Valley?

I. If market interest rates are higher than the coupon rate of the bond, Valley's cost of debt capital will be reduced.
II. Because interest expense is a tax deduction, the cost to Valley is lower than the market yield rate on debt.

(A) I only
(B) II only
(C) Both I and II
(D) Neither I nor II

254. Webster Inc. is planning to use retained earnings to finance anticipated capital expenditures. The beta coefficient for Webster's stock is 1.2, the risk-free rate of interest is 7 percent, and the market return is estimated at 12.4 percent. Using the capital asset pricing model (CAPM), Webster's cost of using retained earnings to finance the capital expenditures is

(A) 13.48 percent
(B) 6.48 percent
(C) 18.48 percent
(D) 8.48 percent

255. Which of the following methods could be used to calculate the cost of common equity capital?

I. Capital asset pricing model
II. Discounted cash flow model

(A) I only
(B) II only
(C) Both I and II
(D) Neither I nor II

256. The stock of Norbert Inc. is selling for $50. The next annual dividend is expected to be $4 and is expected to grow at a rate of 6 percent. The corporate tax rate is 40 percent. What is the firm's cost of common equity?

(A) 14 percent
(B) 8.4 percent
(C) 5.6 percent
(D) 8 percent

257. Which of the following defines the current ratio?

(A) Current assets less current liabilities
(B) Current assets divided by current liabilities
(C) Current liabilities divided by current assets
(D) Current liabilities less current assets

258. Which of the following would have no effect on the current ratio?
   I. Sale of equipment
   II. Declaration of a stock dividend

(A) I only
(B) II only
(C) Both I and II
(D) Neither I nor II

259. During Year 5, Andolini Company's current assets increased by $100,000, current liabilities decreased by $35,000, and net working capital

(A) increased by $65,000
(B) decreased by $65,000
(C) increased by $135,000
(D) decreased by $135,000

260. Return on investment is calculated as the ratio of

(A) operating income to year-end operating assets
(B) operating income to beginning operating assets
(C) operating income to average operating revenue
(D) operating income to average operating assets

261. The following information pertains to Baines Corporation:

	Year 4	Year 5
Operating revenues	$700,000	$900,000
Operating expenses	$550,000	$700,000
Operating assets	$900,000	$1,300,000

What percentage represents the return on investment for Year 5?

(A) 15.38 percent
(B) 18.18 percent
(C) 15.9 percent
(D) 16.7 percent

262. When calculating return on investment for two different companies, which of the following should be used to value the average assets (denominator) so as to minimize the effect of the age of each company's assets and different depreciation methods used?

(A) Replacement cost
(B) Net book value
(C) Gross book value
(D) Liquidation value

263. Which of the following methods of calculating investment return in dollars involves taking net income per the income statement and comparing it to the required rate of return?

  I. Return on investment
  II. Residual income

(A) I only
(B) II only
(C) Both I and II
(D) Neither I nor II

264. Berg Company has two divisions known as J and K. J division has operating income of $150 and total assets of $1,000. K division has operating income of $300 and total assets of $1,200. The required rate of return for Berg is 9 percent. Residual income for the Berg Company would be

(A) $450
(B) $252
(C) $198
(D) $0

265. Ray is the divisional manager of the Henley Corporation. Ray receives a bonus based on 25 percent of the residual income from the division. The results of the division include: divisional revenues, $1,000,000; divisional expenses, $600,000; and divisional assets, $2,000,000. The required rate of return is 15 percent. How much is Ray's bonus?

(A) $25,000
(B) $30,000
(C) $75,000
(D) $100,000

266. Which of the following is/are correct regarding economic value added (EVA)?

I. It is similar to the residual income method in that it measures return in dollars based on net income less required return.
II. With EVA, management can set the hurdle rate or the weighted average cost of capital may be used as the hurdle rate.

(A) I only
(B) II only
(C) Both I and II
(D) Neither I nor II

267. Which of the following measures of investment performance is/are an accrual method rather than a cash method?

I. Net present value
II. Residual income

(A) I only
(B) II only
(C) Both I and II
(D) Neither I nor II

268. Investments that provide a return that exceeds which of the following should continuously add to the value of the firm?

I. Internal rate of return
II. Weighted average cost of capital

(A) I only
(B) II only
(C) Both I and II
(D) Neither I nor II

269. Which of the following would cause a firm to increase the debt in its financial structure?

    I. Decreased economic uncertainty

   II. Increase in corporate tax rates

(A) I only

(B) II only

(C) Both I and II

(D) Neither I nor II

270. Which of the following is/are correct regarding the weighted average cost of capital?

    I. The optimal capital structure is the mix of financing instruments that produces the lowest weighted average cost of capital.

   II. The company's borrowing rate is NOT a component of the weighted average cost of capital.

(A) I only

(B) II only

(C) Both I and II

(D) Neither I nor II

271. Which of the following would lead to a reduction in average inventory?

    I. A decrease in the cost of carrying inventory

   II. An increase in customer demand

(A) I only

(B) II only

(C) Both I and II

(D) Neither I nor II

272. Profitability is measured by the

    I. inventory turnover ratio

   II. debt to total assets ratio

(A) I only

(B) II only

(C) Both I and II

(D) Neither I nor II

273. Liquidity measurements focus on the ability of the company to meet obligations as they come due. Which of the following can be used to measure liquidity?

   I. Quick ratio

  II. Average collection period

(A) I only

(B) II only

(C) Both I and II

(D) Neither I nor II

274. The target capital structure of Kowalski Company is 40 percent debt, 20 percent preferred equity, and 40 percent common equity. The interest rate on debt is 6 percent, the yield on the preferred is 9 percent, the cost of common equity is 12 percent, and the tax rate is 30 percent. Kowalski does not anticipate issuing any new stock. What is Kowalski's weighted average cost of capital?

(A) 10.7 percent

(B) 9 percent

(C) 8.3 percent

(D) 9.8 percent

275. A company's debt to total capital ratio includes which of the following in the denominator?

   I. Interest-bearing debt

  II. Noninterest-bearing debt

(A) I only

(B) II only

(C) Both I and II

(D) Neither I nor II

276. Which of the following actions would have no effect on a company's quick ratio?

   I. Purchasing inventory through the issuance of long-term notes

  II. Selling inventory at a loss

(A) I only

(B) II only

(C) Both I and II

(D) Neither I nor II

277. A corporation obtains a loan of $180,000 at an annual rate of 11 percent. The corporation must keep a compensating balance of 20 percent of any amount borrowed on deposit at the bank but normally does not have a cash balance account with the bank. What is the effective cost of the loan?

(A) 11 percent
(B) 13.5 percent
(C) 13.75 percent
(D) 14 percent

278. Which of the following would NOT be needed to estimate the cost of equity capital for use in determining a firm's weighted average cost of capital?

   I. Current dividends per share
  II. Expected growth rate in earnings per share
 III. Current market price per share of common stock

(A) I only
(B) II and III
(C) I and II
(D) II only

279. Using the discounted cash flow method, estimate the cost of equity capital for a firm with a stock price of $20, an estimated dividend at the end of the first year of $2 per share, and an expected growth rate of 11.5 percent.

(A) 19.5 percent
(B) 11.5 percent
(C) 13.5 percent
(D) 21.5 percent

280. The sale of property, plant, and equipment for an amount of cash less than net book value would result in which of the following?

(A) An increase in working capital and an increase in net income
(B) An increase in working capital and a decrease in net income
(C) A decrease in working capital and a decrease in net income
(D) A decrease in working capital and an increase in net income

281. To measure inventory management performance, the Galkin Company monitors its inventory turnover ratio. Listed are selected data from the company's accounting records:

	Current Year	Prior Year
Sales	$2,375,000	$2,455,000
Cost of goods sold	$1,500,000	Not given
Ending inventory	$350,500	$259,100

If short-term interest rates are 4 percent, what was Galkin Company's inventory turnover at the end of the current period?

(A) 5.45
(B) 4.92
(C) 7.93
(D) 6.31

282. Crown Corporation's budgeted sales and budgeted cost of sales for the coming year are $7,500,000 and $3,800,000, respectively. Short-term interest rates are expected to average 6 percent. If Crown could increase inventory turnover from its current seven times per year to nine times per year, its expected cost savings in the current year would be

(A) $18,236
(B) $9,712
(C) $7,238
(D) $25,333

283. Linden Stove Inc. is a manufacturer. The terms of trade are 4/10, net 30 with a particular supplier of raw materials. What is the cost on an annual basis of NOT taking the discount? Assume a 360-day year.

(A) 75.06 percent
(B) 18.00 percent
(C) 57.07 percent
(D) 37.03 percent

284. Fleming Corporation, a clothing designer, is considering forgoing discounts in order to delay using its cash. Supplier credit terms are 3/10, net 30. Assuming a 360-day year, what is the annual cost of credit if the cash discount is not taken and Fleming pays net 30?

(A) 18.00 percent
(B) 20.25 percent
(C) 35.50 percent
(D) 55.62 percent

285. Which of the following working capital systems arranges for the direct mailing of customers' payments to a bank's post office box and subsequent deposit?

(A) Concentration banking
(B) Lockbox banking
(C) Zero balance account banking
(D) Compensating balances

286. Nadasky Inc. is considering implementing a lockbox collection system at a cost of $50,000 per year. Annual sales are $80 million, and the lockbox system will reduce collection time by three days. If Nadasky can invest funds at 9 percent, should it use the lockbox system? Assume a 360-day year.

(A) No, it produces a loss of $10,000 per year.
(B) No, it produces a loss of $50,000 per year.
(C) Yes, it produces a savings of $60,000 per year.
(D) Yes, it produces a savings of $10,000 per year.

287. Bly Corporation is considering a new cash management system that it estimates can add three days to the disbursement schedule. Average daily cash outflows are $1 million for Bly. Assuming Bly earns 6 percent on excess funds, how much should Bly be willing to pay per year for this cash management system?

(A) $300,000
(B) $180,000
(C) $90,000
(D) $1,000,000

288. A company's cash conversion cycle is calculated as the

(A) sum of the inventory conversion period plus the receivable collection period
(B) sum of the inventory conversion period plus the receivable collection period less the payables deferral period
(C) inventory conversion period less the receivable collection period
(D) receivable collection period less the payables deferral period

289. From one year to the next, which of the following would indicate that a company's cash conversion cycle is improving?
  I. Decrease in inventory conversion period
  II. Decrease in receivable collection period
  III. Decrease in payables deferral period

  (A) I and II
  (B) II and III
  (C) I and III
  (D) I, II, and III

290. Gateway 26 Corporation is trying to maintain inventory for its amusement centers. The CFO noticed that the inventory turnover was higher in Year 2 compared to Year 1 because of a lower average inventory in Year 2 compared to Year 1. This would indicate that the

  (A) inventory conversion period is declining, which is a positive
  (B) inventory conversion period is rising, which is a positive
  (C) inventory conversion period is declining, which is a negative
  (D) inventory conversion period is rising, which is a negative

291. The amount of inventory that a company would tend to hold in stock would decrease as the
  I. cost of running out of stock increases
  II. length of time that goods are in transit decreases

  (A) I only
  (B) II only
  (C) Both I and II
  (D) Neither I nor II

292. Anita's Hallmark Basket needs to determine its reorder point. What is the reorder point if Anita's average sales of Hallmark Cards are 50,000 cards per year, lead time is four weeks, and a safety stock of 750 cards is maintained? Assume Anita's is closed for two weeks during the month of August.

  (A) 1,750
  (B) 4,000
  (C) 4,250
  (D) 4,750

293. Which of the following are correct regarding a switch from a traditional inventory system to a just in time inventory system?

   I. Just in time systems maintain a much smaller level of inventory when compared to traditional systems.

   II. Inventory turnover increases with a switch from traditional to just in time inventory.

   III. Inventory as a percentage of total assets increases with a switch to just in time inventory.

   (A) II and III

   (B) I and II

   (C) I and III

   (D) I, II, and III

294. In inventory management, which of the following would decrease safety stock?

   I. Carrying costs increase

   II. Lower stockout costs

   (A) I only

   (B) II only

   (C) Both I and II

   (D) Neither I nor II

295. The optimal level of inventory is affected by

   I. the time required to receive inventory

   II. the cost per unit of inventory

   III. the cost of placing an order

   IV. the current amount of inventory

   (A) II and III

   (B) I and II

   (C) I, II, III, and IV

   (D) I, II, and III

296. Which of the following would be correct regarding the economic order quantity (EOQ)?

   I. Economic order quantity is a method of inventory control that anticipates orders at the point where carrying costs are nearest to restocking costs.

   II. The objective of EOQ is to minimize total inventory costs.

   (A) I only

   (B) II only

   (C) Both I and II

   (D) Neither I nor II

297. The decision to factor receivables would have which of the following effects?
  I. Increased accounts receivable
  II. Decreased accounts receivable turnover ratio

(A) I only
(B) II only
(C) Both I and II
(D) Neither I nor II

298. A company has ending accounts receivable of $13,000, sales of $105,000, and beginning accounts receivable of $15,000. Cash decreased in the period by $1,900. If total expenses are $20,000, what is the accounts receivable turnover ratio?

(A) 7.50
(B) 8.80
(C) 7.00
(D) 7.05

299. The Paruta Corporation relies on the economic order quantity (EOQ) formula to minimize inventory costs. Which of the following would be expected to remain constant in the EOQ formula?
  I. Carrying cost per unit
  II. Cost of placing an order

(A) I only
(B) II only
(C) Both I and II
(D) Neither I nor II

300. Which of the following would NOT be relevant to economic order quantity (EOQ)?
  I. Purchase price per unit
  II. Annual sales volume

(A) I only
(B) II only
(C) Both I and II
(D) Neither I nor II

301. With regard to the economic order quantity, which of the following costs would be calculated per unit rather than per order?
  I. Ordering cost
  II. Carrying cost
  (A) I only
  (B) II only
  (C) Both I and II
  (D) Neither I nor II

302. The Sneaker Barn sells athletic footwear. One particular model, the Wright Model #5, sells an average of 200 pairs per month and costs $35 per pair. Ordering costs are $50 per order. The carrying cost per unit is $3, which covers insurance on stored goods. The $3 also covers the opportunity costs of carrying the sneakers. Sneaker Barn wishes to minimize ordering and carrying costs. How much is the ideal order level of Wright Model #5 sneakers?

  (A) 178 pairs
  (B) 283 pairs
  (C) 375 pairs
  (D) 421 pairs

CHAPTER **4**

Information Technology

303. An exception report can be described as
    I.   a specific report produced when an error or exception condition occurs
    II. a report that does not currently exist but that needs to be created on demand without having to get a software developer involved

  (A) I only
  (B) II only
  (C) Both I and II
  (D) Neither I nor II

304. In batch processing, grandfather, father, and son files can be used to
    I.   recover from processing problems
    II. retain files off-site for disaster recovery

  (A) I only
  (B) II only
  (C) Both I and II
  (D) Neither I nor II

305. Which of the following is correct regarding batch processing and online real-time processing?

  (A) For batch processing, stored data are constantly current.

  (B) Online real-time transactions are processed on a periodic basis.

  (C) For online real-time processing data to be current, no changes can be made since the last batch update.

  (D) There is no greater level of control necessary for batch processing versus online real-time (online) processing.

306. Which of the following is/are correct regarding an accounting information system (AIS)?
   I. An AIS is best suited to solve problems where there is certainty along with clearly defined reporting requirements.
   II. The first step in an AIS is that transaction data from source documents are entered into the AIS by an end user.
   (A) I only
   (B) II only
   (C) Both I and II
   (D) Neither I nor II

307. Of the steps listed, which of the following is the last step in an AIS?
   (A) The original paper source documents are filed.
   (B) Trial balances are prepared.
   (C) Financial reports are generated.
   (D) The transactions are posted to the general and subsidiary ledgers.

308. Characteristics of centralized processing include
   I. consistency of processing
   II. decreased power and storage needs at the central location
   III. increased local accountability
   (A) I and II
   (B) I and III
   (C) I, II, and III
   (D) I only

309. Centralized processing has which advantage(s) over decentralized processing?
   I. Decreased local accountability
   II. Increased power and storage needs at the central location
   (A) I only
   (B) II only
   (C) Both I and II
   (D) Neither I nor II

310. Business information systems allow a business to perform which of the following functions?
   I. Initiate data
   II. Process data
   (A) I only
   (B) II only
   (C) Both I and II
   (D) Neither I nor II

311. A business information system has which of the following components?
   I. Software
   II. Reports
   III. Hardware
   IV. Data
   V. People

   (A) I, II, III, and IV
   (B) I and III
   (C) I, III, IV, and V
   (D) I, II, III, IV, and V

312. Business information systems allow a business to perform all of the following functions on data EXCEPT
   I. collect
   II. process
   III. store
   IV. initiate
   V. report

   (A) I and IV
   (B) II and III
   (C) IV and V
   (D) IV only

313. Which of the following would NOT be correct regarding production data and test data?
   I. Production and test data are normally stored in the same database.
   II. Access to production data can be considerably less open than access to test data.

   (A) I only
   (B) II only
   (C) Both I and II
   (D) Neither I nor II

314. A general ledger chart of accounts that assigns revenue to the 3000 series and expenses to the 4000 series would be an example of what type of coding?

   (A) Sequential coding
   (B) Block coding
   (C) Group coding
   (D) None of the above

315. Which of the following choices represents the first phase of computer storage?

(A) Databases
(B) Files
(C) Fields
(D) Records

316. A major function of transaction processing is
   I. data storage
   II. data analysis

(A) I only
(B) II only
(C) Both I and II
(D) Neither I nor II

317. Which of the following is/are correct regarding extensible business reporting language (XBRL)?
   I. The Securities and Exchange Commission (SEC) requires public companies to present financial statements and related exhibits using XBRL.
   II. Extensible business reporting language is specifically designed to exchange financial information over the web.

(A) I only
(B) II only
(C) Both I and II
(D) Neither I nor II

318. Which of the following would NOT be correct regarding program modification control software?
   I. Program modification controls include controls that attempt to prevent changes by unauthorized personnel.
   II. Program modification controls track program changes so that there is an exact record of what versions of what programs were running in production at any specific point in time.

(A) I only
(B) II only
(C) Both I and II
(D) Neither I nor II

319. In an IT environment, which of the following duties should NEVER be combined?
  I. Application programmer and systems analyst
  II. Application programmer and systems programmer

  (A) I only
  (B) II only
  (C) Both I and II
  (D) Neither I nor II

320. For software purchased from an outside vendor, which of the following is correct regarding maintenance of the software versus software support?

  (A) Maintenance refers to keeping the system up and running.
  (B) Maintenance includes monitoring the system, determining that a problem has occurred, and fixing or getting around the problem.
  (C) Support refers to keeping the system up and running.
  (D) Support is keeping the system "up to date" with new releases from time to time.

321. Which of the following systems would enable programming teams to work independently on different programs within the same system?
  I. Structured system
  II. Management reporting system
  III. Interactive system

  (A) I and II
  (B) II only
  (C) I and III
  (D) I only

322. Which person sets up and configures computers?

  (A) User
  (B) Software developer
  (C) Network administrator
  (D) Hardware technician

323. Which of the following is a decision support system that uses a what-if technique that asks how a given outcome will change if the original estimates of the model are changed?

  (A) Scenario analysis
  (B) Sensitivity analysis
  (C) Database query applications
  (D) Financial modeling applications

324. Which of the following represents a security risk in an IT environment?
  I. Web crawler
  II. Trojan horse
  III. Backdoor

  (A) I and II
  (B) II and III
  (C) II only
  (D) I, II, and III

325. Which of the following would be responsibilities of the network administrator?
  I. Network maintenance
  II. Design and control of a firm's database
  III. Wireless access

  (A) I and II
  (B) I and III
  (C) I, II, and III
  (D) I only

326. An application programmer is responsible for
  I. writing application programs
  II. maintaining application programs
  III. controlling data entry

  (A) I and II
  (B) II and III
  (C) I only
  (D) I, II, and III

327. For better segregation of duties involving the computer program, which of the following IT jobs is an example of an authorization role that should be segregated from the custody role?

  (A) Librarian
  (B) Computer operator
  (C) Programmer
  (D) Systems analyst

328. Which of the following computer programmers would be responsible for installing, supporting, monitoring, and maintaining the operating system?
   I. Application programmer
   II. System programmer
   (A) I only
   (B) II only
   (C) Both I and II
   (D) Neither I nor II

329. Within the control objectives for information and related technology (COBIT) framework, which of the following would best describe the "reliability" criteria?
   I. To be reliable, the information must be available currently and in the future, and resources must be safeguarded.
   II. To be reliable, information needs to be appropriate to operate the entity.
   (A) I only
   (B) II only
   (C) Both I and II
   (D) Neither I nor II

330. Within the control objectives for information and related technology (COBIT) framework, which of the following would best describe the "integrity" criteria?
   I. Information needs to be accurate, complete, and valid.
   II. Information needs to be low cost without compromising effectiveness.
   (A) I only
   (B) II only
   (C) Both I and II
   (D) Neither I nor II

331. Which of the following are among the five areas for IT governance identified by the control objectives for information and related technology (COBIT) framework?

    I. Strategic alignment

    II. Resource management

    III. Risk management

    IV. Performance measurement

    (A) I, III, and IV

    (B) II, III, and IV

    (C) I, II, and III

    (D) I, II, III, and IV

332. Control objectives for information and related technology (COBIT) defines which of the following as NOT part of IT infrastructure?

    I. Networking and hardware configurations

    II. System software

    (A) I only

    (B) II only

    (C) Both I and II

    (D) Neither I nor II

333. Under the control objectives for information and related technology (COBIT) framework, the "monitor and evaluate" domain relates to

    I. ensuring that directions are followed

    II. providing feedback to information criteria

    (A) I only

    (B) II only

    (C) Both I and II

    (D) Neither I nor II

334. Under the control objectives for information and related technology (COBIT) framework, the "deliver and support" domain relates to

    I. delivery of the IT solution

    II. delivery of the IT service

    (A) I only

    (B) II only

    (C) Both I and II

    (D) Neither I nor II

335. With regard to internal controls, which of the following would remain the same when switching from a manual system to an automated system?
   I. Objectives
   II. Principles
   III. Implementation
   (A) I and II
   (B) II and III
   (C) III only
   (D) I, II, and III

336. Which of the following would normally take responsibility for training staff to use recently purchased software that is being integrated with the company's existing software?
   (A) Computer programmer
   (B) Network administrator
   (C) Systems analyst
   (D) IT supervisor

337. Which of the following types of transaction processing systems would eliminate the need for reconciliation of control accounts and subsidiary ledgers?
   I. Manual systems
   II. Automated systems
   (A) I only
   (B) II only
   (C) Both I and II
   (D) Neither I nor II

338. Executive support systems
   I. provide managers and other users with reports that are typically predefined by management and used to make daily business decisions
   II. process and record routine daily transactions necessary to conduct business
   (A) I only
   (B) II only
   (C) Both I and II
   (D) Neither I nor II

339. In an IT environment, which of the following is/are charged with developing long-range plans and directing application development and computer operations?

(A) Steering committee
(B) Systems analyst
(C) System programmers
(D) End users

340. The Zehra Corporation recently purchased a new payroll program and has finished installing it. Which of the following control actions should be taken by the organization to reduce the risk of incorrect processing due to the implementation of a new system?

I. Segregating transaction authorization, record-keeping, and asset custodial duties
II. Ensuring that overtime is properly authorized
III. Parallel processing transactions for independent verification

(A) I and III
(B) II and III
(C) III only
(D) I, II, and III

341. Which of the following involves using a password or a digital key to scramble a readable (plain text) message into an unreadable (cipher text) message?

(A) Validity check
(B) Encryption
(C) Decryption
(D) Echo check

342. Which of the following would NOT be a form of data security?

I. Password management
II. Data encryption
III. Digital certificates

(A) II only
(B) I only
(C) III only
(D) None of the above

343. Which of the following is true regarding transmitting transactions over a value-added network (VAN) versus over the Internet?

(A) Transactions transmitted over a VAN are batch processed.

(B) In the event of disaster recovery, VANs typically do not archive the data for more than 48 hours.

(C) Transactions transmitted over the Internet are not processed as they occur.

(D) All of the above

344. The Lara Corporation has developed an internal system of managing customer accounts better in order to simplify marketing and sales, provide improved service, and cross-sell products more effectively. Which of the following describes Lara's internal system?

(A) Customer relationship management

(B) Electronic data interchange

(C) Decision support systems

(D) Public key infrastructure

345. Electronic data interchange (EDI) may be transmitted using

   I. a value-added network

   II. the Internet

(A) I only

(B) II only

(C) Both I and II

(D) Neither I nor II

346. Which of the following is/are correct regarding electronic data interchange (EDI)?

   I. The cost of sending EDI transactions using a value-added network (VAN) is greater than the cost of using the Internet.

   II. Electronic data interchange requires strict adherence to a standard data format.

(A) I only

(B) II only

(C) Both I and II

(D) Neither I nor II

347. Which of the following would allow customers to purchase goods over the Internet but would NOT maintain financial privacy?

    I. E-cash

   II. Credit card

  III. Electronic check

  (A) I, II, and III

  (B) II only

  (C) II and III

  (D) I and II

348. In an electronic data interchange (EDI) environment, encoding of data for security purposes is known as

  (A) decoding

  (B) mapping

  (C) encryption

  (D) translation

349. Audit trails in an electronic data interchange (EDI) system should include

    I. activity logs of failed transactions

   II. network and sender/recipient acknowledgments

  (A) I only

  (B) II only

  (C) Both I and II

  (D) Neither I nor II

350. Compared to an electronic data interchange (EDI) environment under a value-added network (VAN), e-commerce transactions over the Internet are

  (A) faster, less expensive, and more secure

  (B) slower, more expensive, and more secure

  (C) slower, less expensive, and less secure

  (D) faster, less expensive, and less secure

351. Which of the following involves having virtual servers available over the Internet for storing hardware and software?

  (A) Domain name warehousing

  (B) Secure socket layer

  (C) Hypertext transfer protocol (HTTP)

  (D) Cloud computing

352. Which of the following is the risk of choosing inappropriate technology?

(A) Strategic risk
(B) Operating risk
(C) Financial risk
(D) Information risk

353. Which of the following statements is/are correct regarding threats in a computerized environment?

  I. In a denial-of-service attack, one computer bombards another computer with a flood of information intended to keep legitimate users from accessing the target computer or network.

  II. Phishing is a program that appears to have a useful function but that contains a hidden and unintended function that presents a security risk.

(A) I only
(B) II only
(C) Both I and II
(D) Neither I nor II

354. Which of the following passwords would be the most difficult to crack?

(A) Matt99
(B) 45561212
(C) y9y9y4j2
(D) 2456dtR5!

355. Which of the following are input controls?

  I. Limit tests
  II. Validity checks

(A) I only
(B) II only
(C) Both I and II
(D) Neither I nor II

Use the following facts to answer **Questions 356–358**.

Check #	Hours	Employee ID #	Net Pay
201	40	943-56-9087	$887.54
202	32	948-65-0901	$612.54
203	10	949-09-4545	$340.32
204	24	991-04-0909	$478.90
205	40	998-01-9002	$567.90
1,015	146		$2,887.20

356. Which of the following control totals represents the batch total?
    (A) 5
    (B) 146
    (C) 1,015
    (D) $2,887.20

357. Which of the following control totals represents the record count?
    (A) 5
    (B) 146
    (C) 1,015
    (D) $2,887.20

358. Which of the following control totals represents the sum of the fifth digit of all five employee ID numbers?
    (A) Batch total
    (B) Hash total
    (C) Record count
    (D) None of the above

359. Electronic access controls include
     I. passwords
    II. firewalls
    (A) I only
    (B) II only
    (C) Both I and II
    (D) Neither I nor II

360. Adler Inc. is preparing a business continuity plan in the event of disaster. Which of the following represents empty floor space where Adler can install whatever hardware is needed in one to three days because the space already contains all electrical requirements?

(A) Warm site
(B) Hot site
(C) Cold site
(D) Purple site

361. Which of the following are correct about a hot site used for disaster recovery?

  I. Hot sites typically involve external providers of floor space and equipment.
  II. Hot sites typically involve off-premises facilities.
  III. Hot sites typically allow for recovery within hours of a disaster.

(A) I and III
(B) II and III
(C) I and II
(D) I, II, and III

362. Which of the following is a privately sponsored form of electronic communication normally used for organizational communications?

(A) Internet
(B) Intranet
(C) Database management system
(D) Compiler

CHAPTER 5

Economics

363. Gross domestic product includes
    I. the value of used goods that have been resold
    II. foreign-owned factories operating within the United States

(A) I only
(B) II only
(C) Both I and II
(D) Neither I nor II

364. Which of the following would remove the effect of inflation as it measures the value of all national output?
    I. Real gross domestic product (GDP)
    II. Nominal GDP

(A) I only
(B) II only
(C) Both I and II
(D) Neither I nor II

365. Fluctuations in economic activity vary in

(A) severity and growth
(B) duration and recession
(C) duration and expansion
(D) severity and duration

366. The peak period of economic growth marks the end of one economic phase and the beginning of another. The peak marks the end of _____ and the beginning of _____.

(A) contraction, growth
(B) expansion, inflation
(C) contraction, expansion
(D) expansion, contraction

367. Which of the following economic cycles is characterized by a rise in demand for goods, a stabilization of corporate profits, and an increase in economic activity?

(A) Peak
(B) Contraction
(C) Expansion
(D) Recovery

368. Which of the following economic cycles is characterized by significant excess production capacity?

(A) Peak
(B) Trough
(C) Expansion
(D) Contraction

369. In a typical recession,
  I. potential output exceeds actual output
  II. real gross domestic product is rising

(A) I only
(B) II only
(C) Both I and II
(D) Neither I nor II

370. Which of the following would be evidence of a potential or even actual recession?
  I. Increasing aggregate demand
  II. Rising unemployment
  III. Falling gross domestic product (GDP)

(A) I, II, and III
(B) II and III
(C) II only
(D) III only

371. Real gross domestic product will rise as a result of

(A) decreasing government purchases
(B) increasing taxes
(C) increasing government purchases
(D) Both A and B

372. Which of the following would be considered expansionary fiscal policy?
   I. An increase in taxes
   II. A decrease in government spending

(A) I only
(B) II only
(C) Both I and II
(D) Neither I nor II

373. An increase in wealth and an increase in overall confidence about the economic outlook will cause

(A) an increase in the cost of capital
(B) a shift in the aggregate demand curve to the left
(C) a shift in the aggregate demand curve to the right
(D) Both A and B

374. As aggregate demand rises,
   I. unemployment decreases
   II. real gross domestic product increases

(A) I only
(B) II only
(C) Both I and II
(D) Neither I nor II

375. In the short run, which of the following would be correct regarding the aggregate supply curve and aggregate demand curve?
   I. Quantity demanded is inversely related to the price level.
   II. Quantity supplied is upward sloping.

(A) I only
(B) II only
(C) Both I and II
(D) Neither I nor II

376. A nation's long-term aggregate supply curve is dependent on
   I. price levels
   II. technology and capital available
   III. labor and materials available

(A) I, II, and III
(B) II and III
(C) I only
(D) None of the above

377. Large decreases in input costs such as direct labor and direct materials would result in

   (A) real gross domestic product (GDP) increasing

   (B) real GDP decreasing

   (C) an increase in price levels

   (D) the aggregate supply curve shifting to the left

378. Real gross domestic product (GDP) per capita is

   I. the measure often used to compare standards of living across countries

   II. calculated by taking real GDP and dividing by population

   (A) I only

   (B) II only

   (C) Both I and II

   (D) Neither I nor II

379. If the US dollar falls in value,

   I. net exports will fall

   II. supply of foreign goods in the US would decrease

   (A) I only

   (B) II only

   (C) Both I and II

   (D) Neither I nor II

380. When inflation occurs,

   I. purchasing power is reduced

   II. those with a fixed obligation are hurt

   (A) I only

   (B) II only

   (C) Both I and II

   (D) Neither I nor II

381. Inflation does NOT

   I. help those on a fixed income

   II. increase the price level

   (A) I only

   (B) II only

   (C) Both I and II

   (D) Neither I nor II

382. An increase in aggregate demand causes

(A) output to rise and the price level to rise
(B) output to rise and the price level to fall
(C) output to fall and the price level to rise
(D) output to fall and the price level to fall

383. A decrease in aggregate supply causes

(A) output to fall and the price level to fall
(B) output to rise and the price level to rise
(C) output to rise and the price level to fall
(D) output to fall and the price level to rise

384. Mismatch of skills and jobs in the economy is an example of what type of unemployment?

(A) Structural unemployment
(B) Cyclical unemployment
(C) Frictional unemployment
(D) Seasonal unemployment

385. Which of the following is correct regarding the type of unemployment and its corresponding cause?

(A) Frictional unemployment is caused by seasonal demand for labor.
(B) Structural unemployment is caused by a time lag that individuals experience between jobs.
(C) Cyclical unemployment is caused by business cycles.
(D) Seasonal unemployment is caused by a mismatch between worker skills and available employment.

386. Unemployment caused by an entire industry being rendered obsolete due to a new invention is known as

(A) seasonal unemployment
(B) structural unemployment
(C) frictional unemployment
(D) cyclical unemployment

387. Gross domestic product can be calculated by the
  I. expenditures approach
  II. income approach
  III. net assets approach
  (A) I only
  (B) I and II
  (C) II only
  (D) I, II, and III

388. When calculating gross domestic product, the expenditures approach uses
  I. net exports
  II. capital investment
  (A) I only
  (B) II only
  (C) Both I and II
  (D) Neither I nor II

389. Business profits and employee compensation are used to calculate gross domestic product under which of the following approaches?
  I. Expenditures approach
  II. Income approach
  (A) I only
  (B) II only
  (C) Both I and II
  (D) Neither I nor II

390. Who sets the discount rate that the central bank charges for loans?
  (A) Commercial banks
  (B) Savings and loans
  (C) Investment banks
  (D) Federal Reserve

391. If government expenditures are $12, imports are $4, exports are $7, investments are $30, and consumption is $16, how much is the gross domestic product, assuming all numbers shown are in the billions?
  (A) $69 billion
  (B) $61 billion
  (C) $58 billion
  (D) $41 billion

392. Using the income approach, calculate gross domestic product for the country of Griffania from the following information:

Consumer spending	$306 billion
Profits to proprietors	$83 billion
Profits to corporations	$119 billion
Employee wages	$305 billion
Net imports	$91 billion
Rental income	$19 billion
Interest income	$80 billion

(A) $912 billion
(B) $606 billion
(C) $697 billion
(D) $515 billion

393. The nation of Pradera wants to measure the value of all final goods and services produced by its residents whether produced within the borders of Pradera or outside Pradera's borders. Which of the following would determine that measure?

(A) Gross domestic product
(B) Net domestic product
(C) Net national product
(D) Gross national product

394. Which of the following measures the rate of increase in the overall price level in the economy?

(A) Prime rate
(B) Discount rate
(C) Nominal rate
(D) Inflation rate

395. Which of the following is a measure of the overall cost of a fixed basket of goods and services purchased by an average household?

(A) Gross domestic product
(B) Gross national product
(C) Consumer price index
(D) Producer price index

396. The consumer price index jumps from 121 in Year 2 to 133.5 in Year 3. What is the annual inflation rate?

(A) 12.5 percent
(B) 10.33 percent
(C) 9.36 percent
(D) 5 percent

397. The consumer price index is measured every

(A) month
(B) year
(C) week
(D) quarter

398. The Federal Reserve's powers include the ability to directly
   I. raise or lower reserve requirements
   II. buy or sell government securities

(A) I only
(B) II only
(C) Both I and II
(D) Neither I nor II

399. Which of the following actions, if taken by the Federal Reserve, would stimulate the economy and expand the money supply?
   I. Reduce the discount rate
   II. Increase reserve requirements
   III. Purchase government securities

(A) I, II, and III
(B) I and II
(C) I and III
(D) II and III

400. Expansionary monetary policy affects the economy through which chain of events?

(A) Interest rates fall, aggregate demand increases, and real gross domestic product (GDP) increases.
(B) Interest rates rise, aggregate demand decreases, and real GDP decreases.
(C) Interest rates rise, aggregate demand increases, and real GDP increases.
(D) Interest rates fall, aggregate demand decreases, and real GDP decreases.

401. Nonmonetary assets whose values increase with inflation include

(A) gold and silver
(B) corporate bonds
(C) state and local government bonds
(D) common stock

402. Which of the following is/are correct regarding perfect competition?
   I. Customers have no real preference about which firm they buy from.
   II. The level of a firm's output is large relative to the industry's total output.

(A) I only
(B) II only
(C) Both I and II
(D) Neither I nor II

403. In monopolistic competition,
   I. few firms make up the entire industry
   II. there are large barriers to entry
   III. there are differentiated products

(A) I only
(B) I and II
(C) III only
(D) I, II, and III

404. A firm in which of the following industries would produce products up to a point where marginal cost equals marginal revenue?
   I. An industry with monopolistic competition
   II. An industry with perfect competition

(A) I only
(B) II only
(C) Both I and II
(D) Neither I nor II

405. Significant barriers to entry and few firms in the marketplace are typical of
   I. monopolistic competition
   II. an oligopoly
   III. perfect competition

(A) II only
(B) I only
(C) I and II
(D) II and III

406. A measure of how sensitive the demand for or the supply of a product is to a change in its price is known as

(A) marginal cost
(B) gross domestic product
(C) elasticity
(D) producer price index

407. If demand is price inelastic, an increase in price will

(A) have no effect on total revenue
(B) decrease total revenue
(C) increase total revenue
(D) None of the above

408. If the Poplar Company raises its price on product G by 20 percent and as a result the quantity demanded drops from 260 units to 200 units, which of the following would be correct?

I. Demand for product G is inelastic.
II. The price increase will result in an overall drop in revenue.

(A) I only
(B) II only
(C) Both I and II
(D) Neither I nor II

409. When demand for a product is unit elastic, which of the following would be correct?

I. A price increase will decrease total revenue.
II. A price decrease will increase total revenue.

(A) I only
(B) II only
(C) Both I and II
(D) Neither I nor II

410. Supply is price inelastic if the absolute price elasticity of supply is

(A) less than 1
(B) greater than or equal to 1
(C) less than or equal to 1
(D) exactly 1

411. If the elasticity of demand for a normal good is estimated to be 1.23, then a 10 percent increase in its price would cause

(A) an increase in quantity demanded of 12.3 percent
(B) total revenue to fall by 10 percent
(C) total revenue to rise by less than 10 percent
(D) a decrease in quantity demanded of 12.3 percent

412. In value chain analysis, the value chain includes
  I. supplier
  II. customer
  III. disposal or recycling
  IV. the firm itself

(A) I, II, and III
(B) II, III, and IV
(C) I, II, and IV
(D) I, II, III, and IV

413. Which of the following would increase the bargaining power of the customer?
  I. Customers are aware that they make up a large volume of a firm's business.
  II. There is much information available to customers about products in the marketplace.
  III. The buyers have high switching costs.

(A) I and III
(B) I and II
(C) I only
(D) I, II, and III

414. Competitive advantage can be defined as which of the following?
  I. Product differentiation
  II. Cost leadership

(A) I only
(B) II only
(C) Both I and II
(D) Neither I nor II

415. Which of the following competitive advantage strategies would fail as a result of brand loyalty?
     I. Differentiation
     II. Cost leadership
     (A) I only
     (B) II only
     (C) Both I and II
     (D) Neither I nor II

416. Which of the following are part of the supply chain operations reference (SCOR) model?
     I. Plan
     II. Deliver
     III. Record
     (A) I and II
     (B) I, II, and III
     (C) II and III
     (D) I and III

417. In a supply chain operations reference (SCOR) model, what type of decision is the selection of vendors?
     (A) Plan
     (B) Source
     (C) Deliver
     (D) Make

418. Assume that product B is a substitute of product A. The fundamental law of demand holds that there is an inverse relationship between the
     I. price of product A and quantity demanded for product B
     II. price of product A and quantity demanded for product A
     III. price of product A and price of product B
     (A) I and III
     (B) II and III
     (C) II only
     (D) I, II, and III

419. Sales of company Q's product R increased 11 percent after company A increased its price on product B from $8 to $9.50. Product R and product B are

(A) complementary goods
(B) substitute goods
(C) independent goods
(D) inferior goods

420. Which of the following would result in an increase in the price of a product?

(A) Increase in quantity demanded and increase in quantity supplied
(B) Increase in quantity demanded and decrease in quantity supplied
(C) Decrease in quantity supplied and decrease in quantity demanded
(D) Decrease in quantity demanded and increase in quantity supplied

421. Goods that are considered normal goods

  I. have a negative elasticity of demand
 II. will increase in demand as income increases

(A) I only
(B) II only
(C) Both I and II
(D) Neither I nor II

422. Demand for a product tends to be price inelastic if

  I. few good substitutes are available for the product
 II. a decline in price results in an increase in total revenue

(A) I only
(B) II only
(C) Both I and II
(D) Neither I nor II

423. If the admission price for a basketball game is raised from $25 to $30, causing attendance to drop from 60,000 to 40,000, the price elasticity of the demand for attending the basketball game is

(A) −2.20
(B) −1.67
(C) 0.60
(D) 2.20

424. When a good is demanded, no matter what the price, demand is described as

(A) perfectly elastic

(B) unit elastic

(C) perfectly inelastic

(D) complementary

425. In a SWOT analysis, which of the following would be correct?

  I. Strengths and weaknesses generally focus on internal factors.

 II. Opportunities and threats generally relate to external factors.

(A) I only

(B) II only

(C) Both I and II

(D) Neither I nor II

426. Which of the following suggests that even if one of two regions is absolutely more efficient in the production of every good than is the other, if each region specializes in the products in which it has greatest relative efficiency, trade will be mutually profitable to both regions?

(A) Comparative advantage

(B) Economies of scale

(C) Law of diminishing returns

(D) High-low method

CHAPTER 6

Management of Risk

427. With regard to the factors that influence production, in the long run,

(A) all costs are broken down between fixed and variable
(B) all costs are fixed
(C) economies of scale will cause production shortages
(D) all costs are variable

428. Porter's five forces affecting a firm's performance include

  I. intensity of firm rivalry
 II. threat of substitute goods
III. threat of new competitors

(A) I and II
(B) I, II, and III
(C) I and III
(D) II and III

429. A just in time inventory system focuses on

  I. minimizing storage costs
 II. eliminating nonvalue-added operations
III. creating specialized labor

(A) I and II
(B) II and III
(C) I, II, and III
(D) II only

430. Which of the following is/are correct regarding conformance and nonconformance costs?
   I. Conformance costs include both prevention and appraisal.
  II. Nonconformance costs include internal and external failure.

(A) I only
(B) II only
(C) Both I and II
(D) Neither I nor II

431. Conformance costs found under the category of prevention include
   I. maintenance
  II. repair
 III. inspection

(A) I and II
(B) I and III
(C) III only
(D) I, II, and III

432. Internal failure costs include
   I. product repair and warranty costs
  II. tooling changes and rework costs

(A) I only
(B) II only
(C) Both I and II
(D) Neither I nor II

433. Which of the following would NOT be a failure cost but a conformance cost?
   I. Repair
  II. Rework

(A) I only
(B) II only
(C) Both I and II
(D) Neither I nor II

434. Which of the following would be a way of seeking radical change by ignoring the current process and instead starting from the beginning to design a different way of achieving the end goal and/or product?
   I. Process management
  II. Process reengineering

(A) I only
(B) II only
(C) Both I and II
(D) Neither I nor II

435. Within project management, which of the following is responsible for project administration on a day-to-day basis, including identifying and managing internal and external stakeholder expectations?

(A) Project sponsor
(B) Project manager
(C) Steering committee
(D) Project members

436. Within project management, the project manager reports to the

(A) project sponsor
(B) project members
(C) steering committee
(D) board of directors

437. Within project management, which of the following parties is responsible for overall project delivery?

(A) Project members
(B) Project manager
(C) Board of directors
(D) Project sponsor

438. Within project management, the project sponsor should communicate project needs to the
  I. executive steering committee
  II. board of directors

(A) I only
(B) II only
(C) Both I and II
(D) Neither I nor II

439. Which of the following is known as the increased dispersion and integration of the world's economies and is often objectively measured as the growth in world trade as a percentage of gross domestic product?

(A) Outsourcing
(B) Off-shore activities
(C) Globalization
(D) Exports as a percentage of imports

440. Compared to long-term financing, short-term financing
    I. increases credit risk
    II. decreases profitability
    (A) I only
    (B) II only
    (C) Both I and II
    (D) Neither I nor II

441. *Diversifiable risk* may also be referred to as
    I. unique risk
    II. unsystematic risk
    (A) I only
    (B) II only
    (C) Both I and II
    (D) Neither I nor II

442. Which of the following is correct regarding default and credit risk?
    (A) The lender's default risk is based on the borrower's default risk.
    (B) The lender's default risk is based on the borrower's credit risk.
    (C) The lender's credit risk is based on the borrower's default risk.
    (D) The lender's credit risk is based on the lender's default risk.

443. Which of the following relates to purchasing power risk?
    (A) The fluctuation in the value of a "financial asset" when interest rates change
    (B) The risk that price levels will change and affect asset values
    (C) The ability to sell a temporary investment in a short period of time without significant price concessions
    (D) A general category of risk that includes default risk and interest rate risk

444. Wildwood Corporation issued bonds four years ago. If the _____ interest rate _____, the market value of each Wildwood corporate bond will _____.
    (A) coupon, increases, decrease
    (B) market, increases, increase
    (C) market, increases, decrease
    (D) market, decreases, decrease

445. If a US company has net cash outflows in a foreign currency, which of the following is correct?

(A) The US company would benefit from a drop in value of the foreign currency.

(B) The US company would benefit from an increase in value of the foreign currency.

(C) The US company would suffer a loss from a decrease in value of the foreign currency.

(D) The appreciation or depreciation of the foreign currency would be irrelevant.

446. A US firm that has cash flows in a foreign currency will suffer an economic loss if

  I. the foreign currency appreciates and the US firm has net cash inflows

  II. the US firm has net cash outflows and the foreign currency depreciates

(A) I only

(B) II only

(C) Both I and II

(D) Neither I nor II

447. The decision to exercise a call option would NOT be based on

  I. strike price

  II. call premium

  III. market price of the underlying security

(A) I and II

(B) II and III

(C) II only

(D) I only

448. Compared to US Treasury bonds, equity securities and corporate bonds, respectively, are

(A) more risky, less risky

(B) less risky, more risky

(C) less risky, less risky

(D) more risky, more risky

449. Which of the following is correct regarding the US dollar?

(A) A strong US dollar makes domestic goods relatively more expensive than imported goods.

(B) A strong US dollar is better for a US company than a weak US dollar.

(C) A weak US dollar makes imported goods relatively cheaper than domestic goods.

(D) A weak US dollar makes domestic goods more expensive than imported goods.

450. Which of the following would happen if the price of the British pound were to increase relative to the US dollar?

 I. The British pound would buy more British goods.

 II. The British pound would buy more US goods.

(A) I only

(B) II only

(C) Both I and II

(D) Neither I nor II

451. As a general rule, which of the following domestic entities would be subject to foreign currency translation risk?

 I. A US entity whose foreign operations are limited to exporting goods to Canada

 II. A US entity who owns a Japanese subsidiary

(A) I only

(B) II only

(C) Both I and II

(D) Neither I nor II

452. Wright International is a US firm that typically exports goods to Japan. Since the international receivables are denominated in yen, they are subject to fluctuating currency rates. To mitigate this risk, Wright sometimes purchases put options to protect against loss from a decline in the yen. The put premium is NOT relevant to the

 I. decision to exercise the option

 II. calculation of gain or loss on the exercise of the put option

(A) I only

(B) II only

(C) Both I and II

(D) Neither I nor II

453. Olympic Enterprises Inc. owns recreation centers with virtual reality games. The entity constantly needs to upgrade its arcades and fun centers with the latest releases. The bank requires a compensating balance of 15 percent on a $100,000 loan. If the stated annual interest rate is 6 percent, what is the effective cost of the loan to Olympic Enterprises?

(A) 7.05 percent
(B) 6.69 percent
(C) 6 percent
(D) 7.8 percent

454. Hayes Corporation is a US manufacturer of musical instruments. Which of the following risks is Hayes subject to if it uses its own cumulative earnings in capitalizing its operations?

  I. Financial risk
 II. Business risk
III. Interest rate risk

(A) I only
(B) II only
(C) I and II
(D) I, II, and III

455. The required rate of return is generally computed as the risk-free rate of return plus a number of risk premium adjustments, including the maturity risk premium. Which of the following is/are correct regarding the interest rate risk?

  I. Interest rate risk is an adjustment to the risk-free rate of return and is the additional compensation demanded by lenders for bearing the risk that the issuer of the security will fail to pay the interest or fail to repay the principal.
 II. Interest rate risk is an adjustment to the risk-free rate of return and is the compensation investors demand for bearing risk.
III. Interest rate risk is directly related to the term to maturity.

(A) I, II, and III
(B) III only
(C) II and III
(D) II only

456. Donruss Corporation is considering investing in a new project known as the Topps project. To evaluate the Topps project, Donruss management has developed the following cash flow projections and related probabilities:

Present Value of Future Cash Flows	Probability of Occurrence
$100,000	0.1
$600,000	0.3
$900,000	0.2
$300,000	0.4

What is the expected return for the Topps project?
(A) $180,000
(B) $220,000
(C) $490,000
(D) $480,000

457. A professional football team, the Gopher Gulch Lions play a 16-game season and have developed a model to predict December sales of team logo apparel based on the previous year's wins and losses.

Unit Sales	Team Record	Probability
5,000	5 wins or fewer	0.1
11,000	6–8 wins	0.4
30,000	9–11 wins	0.3
100,000	12 or more wins	0.2

What sales volume, in units, would the Gopher Gulch Lions anticipate, using the expected value method?
(A) 35,100
(B) 36,900
(C) 33,900
(D) 34,200

458. Which of the following would generally result when a corporation, about to issue new bonds, agrees to a debt covenant?
 I. The coupon rate of new corporate bonds would be increased.
 II. The company's bond rating would be lowered.
(A) I only
(B) II only
(C) Both I and II
(D) Neither I nor II

459. Immediately after raising capital, what is the effect (increase or decrease) on the debt equity ratio if the capital raised is from the sale of long-term bonds versus the sale of common stock?

	Long-Term Bonds	**Common Stock**
(A)	Increase	Decrease
(B)	Increase	Increase
(C)	Increase	No effect
(D)	Decrease	Increase

460. Which of the following best describes P/E ratio?

(A) Market price per share divided by net income
(B) Net income (minus preferred dividend) divided by common shares outstanding
(C) Market price per share divided by earnings per share
(D) Market price per share beginning of the year less market price per share end of the year divided by net income

461. Which of the following is/are correct regarding the P/E ratio?

I. The P/E ratio measures the amount that investors are willing to pay for each dollar of earnings per share.
II. Lower P/E ratios generally indicate that investors are anticipating more growth and are bidding up the price of the shares in advance of performance.

(A) I only
(B) II only
(C) Both I and II
(D) Neither I nor II

462. Sudbury Education Inc. has a payout of 30 percent and a forecasted growth rate of 9 percent. If investors require a 11 percent rate of return on their investment, what is the estimated P/E multiple on this stock?

(A) 14×
(B) 15×
(C) 17×
(D) 19×

463. Which of the following types of security holders do NOT receive income when dividends are declared by the board of directors?

I. Preferred equity security holders
II. Debt security holders

(A) I only
(B) II only
(C) Both I and II
(D) Neither I nor II

464. Which of the following is/are correct regarding the constant growth dividend discount model?
   I. The stock price will grow at a faster rate than the dividend.
   II. The growth rate is less than the discount rate.

   (A) I only
   (B) II only
   (C) Both I and II
   (D) Neither I nor II

465. An investor is considering purchasing shares in a company with a dividend of $4 per share. If a zero growth model is used and 10 percent represents the desired return, how much should the stock sell for?

   (A) $40
   (B) $160
   (C) $16
   (D) $80

466. Assume that Aragona Corporation pays a dividend of $4 per share on its common stock and is expected to grow at 5 percent per year. Prager, an investor, wants to invest in Aragona and earn a 20 percent annual return. How much is Prager willing to pay for Aragona stock today?

   (A) $15
   (B) $21.25
   (C) $25.50
   (D) $28

467. Orange Corporation has a P/E ratio of 20 and its earnings in the current year are $10 per share. In the coming years, earnings of $18 per share are expected. What is the anticipated share price of Orange?

   (A) $200
   (B) $360
   (C) $420
   (D) $480

468. Griffin is studying behavioral corporate finance to learn how management behavior can distort judgment. Which of the following would describe the behavioral characteristic known as confirmation bias?
  I. A manager's belief that results will generally be positive
  II. Managers ignore data that challenge their ideas and instead rely on data that agree with their conclusions

  (A) I only
  (B) II only
  (C) Both I and II
  (D) Neither I nor II

469. Managers tend to rely heavily on a ratio of sales per share when the company
  I. has regular earnings
  II. is a start-up

  (A) I only
  (B) II only
  (C) Both I and II
  (D) Neither I nor II

470. Which of the following ratios would NOT be meaningful if there were a loss or if earnings were extremely small?
  I. P/E ratio
  II. Price to sales ratio

  (A) I only
  (B) II only
  (C) Both I and II
  (D) Neither I nor II

471. According to behavioral finance, what is a financial manager suffering from if the manager believes that his or her actions will cause earnings to increase and market prices to remain in proportion to increased earnings?
  I.   Confirmation bias
  II. Excessive optimism
  III. Illusion of control

  (A) I and II
  (B) II and III
  (C) III only
  (D) I and III

CHAPTER **7**

Corporate Governance

472. The Sarbanes-Oxley Act addresses the problems related to inadequate board oversight by requiring public companies to have an
   I. audit committee
   II. annual audit for all issuers

(A) I only
(B) II only
(C) Both I and II
(D) Neither I nor II

473. According to the Sarbanes-Oxley Act, corporate responsibility for financial reports includes the CEO and CFO certifying the
   I. annual report
   II. quarterly reports

(A) I only
(B) II only
(C) Both I and II
(D) Neither I nor II

474. According to the Sarbanes-Oxley Act, corporate responsibility for financial reports includes the CEO and CFO certifying that they have reviewed the report and that the report does NOT
   I. contain untrue statements
   II. omit material information

(A) I only
(B) II only
(C) Both I and II
(D) Neither I nor II

475. Under the Sarbanes-Oxley Act, which of the following would be considered an enhanced financial disclosure?

    I. Contingent obligations such as pending lawsuits where the loss has NOT been accrued

   II. Disclosures of transactions between investor and investee accounted for under the consolidated method

  (A) I only
  (B) II only
  (C) Both I and II
  (D) Neither I nor II

476. Under the Sarbanes-Oxley Act, which of the following are enhanced disclosures required in periodic reports?

    I. All correcting adjustments identified by the independent auditor

   II. Relationships with unconsolidated subsidiaries

  III. Material off–balance sheet transactions

  (A) I and II
  (B) I and III
  (C) II and III
  (D) I, II, and III

477. The Sarbanes-Oxley Act requires that the management report on internal control include

    I. a statement of management's responsibilities for establishing and maintaining adequate internal controls

   II. a conclusion about the effectiveness of the company's internal controls

  (A) I only
  (B) II only
  (C) Both I and II
  (D) Neither I nor II

478. The Sarbanes-Oxley Act requires that the management report on internal control include

    I. a statement that there are no disagreements between management and the auditor as to the effectiveness of internal controls

   II. a statement that the independent auditor has attested and reported on management's evaluation of internal controls

  (A) I only
  (B) II only
  (C) Both I and II
  (D) Neither I nor II

479. The Sarbanes-Oxley Act requires that the officers of a corporation be held accountable to a code of ethics. According to the act, codifications of ethical standards should include provisions for
   I. full, fair, accurate, and timely disclosure in periodic financial statements
  II. honest and ethical conduct

(A) I only
(B) II only
(C) Both I and II
(D) Neither I nor II

480. According to the Sarbanes-Oxley Act, which of the following statements would be correct regarding an issuer's audit committee financial expert?
   I. The issuer's current outside CPA firm's audit partner would be a good choice to be the audit committee financial expert.
  II. The audit committee financial expert should be the issuer's audit committee chairperson to enhance internal control.

(A) I only
(B) II only
(C) Both I and II
(D) Neither I nor II

481. According to the Sarbanes-Oxley Act, which of the following statements is/are correct regarding an issuer's audit committee financial expert?
   I. If an issuer does not have an audit committee financial expert, the issuer must disclose the reason why the role is not filled.
  II. The issuer must fill the role with an individual who has been a financial expert before.

(A) I only
(B) II only
(C) Both I and II
(D) Neither I nor II

482. Qualifications for which of the following is a judgmental issue typically made by the board of directors?
   I. Serving on the audit committee
  II. Being designated the audit committee financial expert

(A) I only
(B) II only
(C) Both I and II
(D) Neither I nor II

483. According to the Committee of Sponsoring Organizations (COSO), within the control environment, management's operating style relates to
   I. work ethic
   II. commitment to effective financial reporting
(A) I only
(B) II only
(C) Both I and II
(D) Neither I nor II

484. According to the Sarbanes-Oxley Act, which of the following individuals would be considered automatically qualified for the position of audit committee financial expert?
   I. Anyone with a CPA certificate
   II. A full-time tenured professor of accounting at a well-known university who has already earned a PhD
(A) I only
(B) II only
(C) Both I and II
(D) Neither I nor II

485. Within the Committee of Sponsoring Organizations (COSO) framework of control environment, management's operating style relates to
   I. recruitment of employees
   II. retention and evaluation of employees
(A) I only
(B) II only
(C) Both I and II
(D) Neither I nor II

486. For compensation and promotion purposes, Fessler Corporation evaluates employees who are responsible for financial reporting on how well they fulfill those responsibilities. The company's policies support the idea that
   I. human resources practices should be designed to facilitate effective internal control over financial reporting
   II. management's philosophy and operating style support achieving effective internal control over financial reporting
(A) I only
(B) II only
(C) Both I and II
(D) Neither I nor II

487. The existence of a published code of ethics and a periodic acknowledgment that ethical values are understood is evidence of

    I. the development of ethical values and ensuring that those values are understood and taken seriously

    II. the board of directors understanding and exercising oversight responsibility related to financial reporting and related internal control

(A) I only

(B) II only

(C) Both I and II

(D) Neither I nor II

488. Broad Corporation has a corporate compliance program that allows employees the option of anonymously reporting violations of laws, rules, regulations, or policies or other issues of abuse through a hotline. Reported issues are reviewed by the internal auditor and either immediately forwarded to the CEO or summarized and reported to the CEO each month. The program also provides opportunities to report through supervisory channels and includes a biannual training class that all employees must complete. The corporate compliance program demonstrates which of the following?

    I. Sound integrity and ethical values are developed and understood and set the standard of conduct for financial reporting.

    II. Management and employees are assigned appropriate levels of authority and responsibility to facilitate effective internal control over financial reporting.

(A) I only

(B) II only

(C) Both I and II

(D) Neither I nor II

489. Active engagement by an audit committee in representing the board of directors relative to all matters of internal and external audits is evidence of

    I. the board's understanding of its oversight responsibility over financial reporting

    II. the need for an organizational structure to support effective internal control over financial reporting

(A) I only

(B) II only

(C) Both I and II

(D) Neither I nor II

490. According to the Committee of Sponsoring Organizations (COSO), which of the following would anticipate that matters affecting the achievement of financial reporting are communicated with outside parties?

(A) Internal control information
(B) Internal communication
(C) Variance analysis
(D) External communication

491. According to the Committee of Sponsoring Organizations (COSO) framework, variance analysis primarily supports

(A) internal control information
(B) external control communication
(C) internal control communication
(D) effective financial reporting

492. According to the Committee of Sponsoring Organizations (COSO) of the Treadway Commission, reporting that triggers prompt exception resolution, root cause analysis, and control updates illustrates the principle of

(A) internal control information
(B) financial reporting information
(C) internal communications
(D) external communications

493. According to the Committee of Sponsoring Organizations (COSO) of the Treadway Commission, which of the following components of the internal control integrated framework would address an entity's timely reporting of identified internal control deficiencies?

   I. Control environment
  II. Monitoring

(A) I only
(B) II only
(C) Both I and II
(D) Neither I nor II

494. According to the Committee of Sponsoring Organizations (COSO) enterprise risk management (ERM) framework, which of the following would involve the determination of the likelihood and impact of events on the achievement of objectives?

(A) Control activities
(B) Risk assessment
(C) Inherent risk
(D) Residual risk

495. A response to risk that involves the diversification of product offerings rather than the elimination of product offerings is called risk

(A) acceptance
(B) avoidance
(C) reduction
(D) sharing

496. Insuring against losses or entering into joint ventures to address risk is known as risk

(A) acceptance
(B) avoidance
(C) reduction
(D) sharing

497. According to the Committee of Sponsoring Organizations (COSO), which of the following would be an operations objective?
  I. Maintaining adequate staffing to keep overtime and benefit costs within budget
  II. Maintaining direct labor cost variances within published guidelines
  III. Maintaining accounting principles that conform to US GAAP

(A) I and III
(B) I, II, and III
(C) II and III
(D) I and II

498. The control activities component of the enterprise risk management (ERM) framework includes key elements that relate to
  I. the policies and procedures that ensure appropriate responses to identified risks
  II. integrity and ethical values

(A) I only
(B) II only
(C) Both I and II
(D) Neither I nor II

499. According to the Committee of Sponsoring Organizations (COSO), which of the following would be included in the "tone at the top"?
  I. Demonstrate appropriate behavior by example
  II. Ensure that internal controls continue to operate effectively

(A) I only
(B) II only
(C) Both I and II
(D) Neither I nor II

500. The International Professional Practices Framework (IPPF) organizes the authoritative guidance published by the Institute of Internal Auditors into which of the following categories?

I. Mandatory guidance

II. Strongly recommended guidance

III. Guidance currently under consideration

(A) I, II, and III

(B) II and III

(C) I and III

(D) I and II

Bonus Questions

501. Which of the following International Professional Practices Framework (IPPF) authoritative guidance regarding internal auditing would be considered mandatory guidance?

I. International standards on internal auditing

II. Code of ethics

(A) I only

(B) II only

(C) Both I and II

(D) Neither I nor II

502. Which of the following International Professional Practices Framework (IPPF) authoritative guidance regarding internal auditing would be considered strongly recommended but not mandatory?

I. Practice guides

II. Position papers

III. Code of ethics

(A) I and III

(B) I and II

(C) I only

(D) I, II, and III

503. The code of ethics issued as part of the International Professional Practices Framework (IPPF) for internal auditors provides principles and rules of conduct under how many different headings?

(A) 4

(B) 5

(C) 6

(D) 10

504. According to the code of ethics for internal auditors, which of the following is presumed to be impaired if an internal auditor provides assurance services for an activity for which the internal auditor had responsibility within the previous year?

(A) Integrity
(B) Objectivity
(C) Confidentiality
(D) Competency

505. According to the Committee of Sponsoring Organizations (COSO) framework, issued by the Treadway Commission, the various components of internal control are used by an entity to help it achieve its objectives. According to the COSO framework, internal control consists of how many interrelated components?

(A) 3
(B) 4
(C) 5
(D) 6

Chapter 1: Operations Management

1. (B) II is correct. Nonfinancial measures include number of days missed due to workplace accidents, an example of nonfinancial performance. Nonfinancial measures are attention getters without the use of dollar figures. Another example of a nonfinancial performance measure would be the number of defective goods manufactured. I is wrong. Gross margin is a measure of financial performance.

2. (C) I and II are correct. Total productivity ratios are nonfinancial measures. Total productivity ratios compare the value of all output to the value of all input. Partial productivity ratios are also nonfinancial measures. Partial productivity ratios compare the value of all output to the value of just some input—for example, the value of all output to the value of direct materials input. A different partial productivity ratio would compare the value of all output with the value of just direct labor input. Productivity ratios measure outputs achieved in relation to the inputs of production. Productivity ratios measure efficiency.

3. (A) I is correct. A control chart is a measure of nonfinancial performance that is considered an internal benchmark (see Figure 1). A control chart shows the performance of a particular manufacturing process in relation to acceptable upper and lower limits of error, or deviation. Control charts show if there is a trend of improved quality performance or if there is a trend of more error. II is wrong. A total productivity ratio is a measure of nonfinancial performance and is considered an external rather than an internal benchmark.

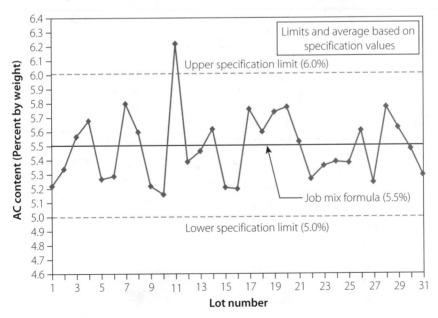

Figure 1 Sample control chart

4. (C) I and II are correct. Fishbone diagrams are considered internal benchmarks (see Figure 2). Fishbone diagrams describe a process, the contributions to the process, and the potential problems that could occur at each phase of the process. Fishbone diagrams identify a quality control problem and track the defect back to the source. A Pareto diagram also is considered an internal benchmark (see Figure 3). A Pareto diagram is used to determine quality control problems that occur most frequently so they can receive the more urgent attention and be corrected first. Then the next most frequent problem can be corrected.

5. (A) I is correct. A control chart shows the performance of a particular process in relation to acceptable upper and lower limits of deviation. Processes are designed to ensure that performance consistently falls within the acceptable range of error. II is wrong. A fishbone diagram describes a process, the contributions to the process, and the potential problems that could occur at each phase of a process. The fishbone diagram attempts to track the problem back to the source rather than to show the upper and lower limits of acceptable error.

6. (B) A Pareto diagram is used to determine quality control problems that occur most frequently so they can receive the more urgent attention and be corrected first; then the next most frequent problem can be corrected, and so on. (A) is wrong. While the control chart for an individual ride would show if there is a trend of improved quality performance for that ride or if there is a trend of more shutdowns with that specific ride, the control chart would not show which ride had the most shutdowns. (C) is wrong. The fishbone diagram would describe the amusement ride and attempt to track the shutdown back

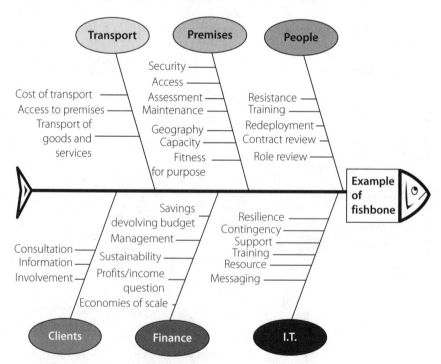

Figure 2 Sample fishbone diagram

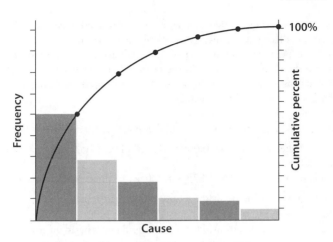

Figure 3 Sample Pareto diagram

to the source. Was it a software problem or equipment malfunction? A fishbone diagram would not show which ride had the most shutdowns.

7. (C) Honest John Inc. uses a transaction marketing practice. A transaction marketing practice emphasizes a single sale with no further interaction with the customer required. A retailer like Honest John that is following such practices believes that customers are attracted to low prices and will likely return based on price only. (A) is wrong. Interaction-based relationship marketing views the sale as the beginning of an ongoing relationship with the customer. The customer will return, thus providing more revenue to the firm as the relationship grows. (B) is wrong. Network marketing attempts to build sales through referrals. (D) is wrong. Database marketing involves targeting ads to specific customer profiles.

8. (D) II is correct. Interaction-based relationship marketing says that sales further relationships, thereby driving more sales. With interaction-based marketing, the sale is just the start of the relationship with the potential of continued revenue through service and parts. I is wrong. Database marketing uses data as the foundation for identifying target markets. III is wrong. Transaction marketing says that customers are attracted to low prices and will return based only on price.

9. (B) II is correct. Competitive commission plans tend to emphasize current compensation; the employee can take the commission or bonus and leave. I is wrong. Future compensation involves stock options since the employee needs to continue in employment into the future to earn the shares represented by the options.

10. (A) I is correct. Product costs are inventoriable. They are assets and remain on the balance sheet until the product is sold. II is wrong. Period costs are expensed immediately in the period incurred.

11. (C) Inventoriable costs include direct materials and direct labor. Both costs would remain on the balance sheet until the product is sold.

12. (C) I and II are correct. Activities that cause costs to increase as the activity increases are known as cost drivers. Cost drivers can be financial or nonfinancial. An example of a nonfinancial cost driver is the number of direct labor hours. As employees work more hours, more overhead cost is incurred in the factory. Machine hours are another example of a nonfinancial cost driver used to allocate overhead to a product. As the machinery runs, utility cost is being generated in the factory.

13. (B) Using direct labor hours, the overhead applied calculation is as follows:

$75,000 budgeted overhead ÷ 20,000 budgeted direct labor hours = $3.75 per direct labor hour
Overhead applied to the job = $3.75 × 1,200 actual direct labor hours, or $4,500

Overhead is applied using budgeted figures rather than actual.

14. (B) II is correct. A predetermined factory overhead rate is based on estimates. Estimated figures are used because actual cost figures are not known at the beginning of a period. Estimated variable overhead costs divided by estimated activity level equals the predetermined factory overhead rate. The numerator is the estimated dollar amount of overhead; the denominator may be estimated machine hours or estimated direct labor hours. Therefore, the predetermined factory overhead rate is based on estimates rather than actual figures.

15. (B) A predetermined factory overhead rate is based on estimates. Estimated figures are used because actual cost figures are not known at the beginning of a period. A predetermined factory overhead rate could be obtained by dividing estimated variable overhead costs by the number of estimated machine hours.

16. (C) Prime costs are the sum of direct labor and direct materials:

Direct labor	$16,000
Direct materials	+ $4,000
Prime costs	$20,000

17. (A) Total product costs are the sum of direct materials, direct labor, and factory overhead applied. To estimate the total product costs on the proposed job, prime costs were already calculated in Question 16 as the sum of direct labor and direct materials:

Direct labor	$16,000
Direct materials	+ $4,000
Prime costs	$20,000

Add in overhead applied of $8,000, calculated as follows (the estimated overhead application rate is calculated from the budgeted information given):

Indirect labor	$90,000
Replacement parts for factory machinery	+ $70,000
Total budgeted overhead	$160,000

$160,000 ÷ Cost driver = Applied overhead

The cost driver for this question is the direct labor hours for the proposed job, or 40,000 hours.

$160,000 ÷ 40,000 hours = $4 per direct labor hour

For every hour of direct labor, $4 is applied to overhead.

2,000 hours × $4 rate	$8,000
Prime costs	+ $20,000
Total estimated product cost of the job	$28,000

18. (A) In the relevant range, fixed costs are constant in total but decrease per unit as production levels increase. The relevant range refers to the short term rather than the long term. In the short term, costs can be broken down between fixed and variable. Variable costs change with production. In the long term, all costs are considered variable because even fixed costs like rent eventually become variable (e.g., leases eventually expire).

19. (C) I and II are correct. Variable costs per unit remain unchanged in the relevant range. Variable costs increase in total as unit volume increases.

20. (D) The amount of direct materials used is calculated as follows:

Beginning inventory, direct materials	$134,000
Purchases during March	+ $190,000
Purchase returns and allowances	− $1,000
Transportation in	+ $2,000
Total direct materials available	$325,000
Ending inventory, direct materials	− $124,000
Direct materials used during March	$201,000

21. (C) Prime costs are calculated as follows:

Step 1—Compute direct materials used.

Beginning inventory, direct materials	$134,000
Purchases during March	+ $190,000
Purchase returns and allowances	− $1,000
Transportation in	+ $2,000
Total direct materials available	$325,000
Ending inventory, direct materials	− $124,000
Direct materials used during March	$201,000

Step 2—Add direct labor.

| Direct labor | + $200,000 |
| Total prime costs | $401,000 |

22. (D) Step 1—Compute direct materials used.

Beginning inventory, direct materials	$134,000
Purchases during March	+ $190,000
Purchase returns and allowances	− $1,000
Transportation in	+ $2,000
Total direct materials available	$325,000
Ending inventory, direct materials	− $124,000
Direct materials used during March	$201,000

Step 2—Add direct labor.

Direct labor	+ $200,000
Total prime costs	$401,000

Step 3—Apply overhead.

$0.40 × $200,000 direct labor dollars	+ $80,000
Total manufacturing costs incurred for March	$481,000

Note that actual overhead of $165,000 is irrelevant (until year-end).

23. (C) The calculation is as follows:

Step 1—Compute direct materials used.

Beginning inventory, direct materials	$134,000
Purchases during March	+ $190,000
Purchase returns and allowances	− $1,000
Transportation in	+ $2,000
Total direct materials available	$325,000
Ending inventory, direct materials	− $124,000
Direct materials used during March	$201,000

Step 2—Add direct labor.

Direct labor	+ $200,000
Total prime costs	$401,000

Step 3—Apply overhead.

$0.40 × $200,000 direct labor dollars	+ $80,000
Total manufacturing costs incurred	$481,000

Step 4—Add beginning work in process.

Beginning work in process	+ $230,000
Total manufacturing costs available for March	$711,000

Note that manufacturing costs available differs from manufacturing costs incurred by the amount of beginning work-in-process inventory of $230,000.

24. (B) Cost of goods manufactured is $461,000, calculated as follows:

Step 1—Compute direct materials used.

Beginning inventory, direct materials	$134,000
Purchases during March	+ $190,000
Purchase returns and allowances	− $1,000
Transportation in	+ $2,000
Total direct materials available	$325,000
Ending inventory, direct materials	− $124,000
Direct materials used during March	$201,000

Step 2—Add direct labor.

Direct labor	+ $200,000
Total prime costs	$401,000

Step 3—Apply overhead.

$0.40 × $200,000 direct labor dollars	+ $80,000
Total manufacturing costs incurred	$481,000
Beginning work in process	+ $230,000
Total manufacturing costs for March	$711,000
Ending work in process	− $250,000
Cost of goods manufactured	$461,000

25. (C) The first step in calculating cost of goods sold for a manufacturer is to calculate cost of goods manufactured. Cost of goods manufactured is $461,000, calculated as follows:

Step 1—Compute direct materials used.

Beginning inventory, direct materials	$134,000
Purchases during March	+ $190,000
Purchase returns and allowances	− $1,000
Transportation in	+ $2,000
Total direct materials available	$325,000
Ending inventory, direct materials	− $124,000
Direct materials used during March	$201,000

Step 2—Add direct labor.

Direct labor	+ $200,000
Total prime costs	$401,000

Step 3—Apply overhead.

$0.40 × $200,000 direct labor dollars	+ $80,000
Total manufacturing costs incurred	$481,000
Beginning work in process	+ $230,000
Total manufacturing costs for March	$711,000
Ending work in process	− $250,000
Cost of goods manufactured	$461,000

Once cost of goods manufactured is known, cost of goods sold can easily be determined by adding beginning finished goods and subtracting ending finished goods.

$461,000 + $120,000 (beginning finished goods) − $110,000 (ending finished goods) = $471,000 (cost of goods sold)

26. (A) For a manufacturing operation, cost of goods sold is equal to cost of goods manufactured plus beginning finished goods minus ending finished goods.

27. (D) A simple example to calculate cost of goods manufactured from total manufacturing costs is as follows:

Total manufacturing costs	10
Beginning work in process	+ 1
Ending work in process	− 5
Cost of goods manufactured	6

28. (D) Cost of goods manufactured plus beginning finished goods less ending finished goods equals cost of goods sold.

29. (B) Since manufacturing overhead is applied on the basis of direct labor dollars, the total of the direct labor dollars for September must first be determined:

$1,000 + $4,500 + $2,000 = $7,500

Manufacturing overhead is applied at the rate of 200 percent, so $15,000 was applied for the month of September (200% × $7,500 = $15,000). Actual manufacturing overhead for September was $17,500, so manufacturing overhead was underapplied by $2,500 ($17,500 − $15,000). In a factory overhead control T account, actual costs are debits. Overhead applied is credited. A debit balance at the end means underapplied actual costs were higher. In this case actual costs were higher than budget by $2,500.

Factory Overhead Control	
Actual	**Applied**
$17,500	$15,000

Ending balance $2,500

30. (B) II is correct. The cost of indirect materials used increases the factory overhead control account and decreases materials control. All actual overhead costs are debited to the overhead control T account. I is wrong. Overhead applied is based on estimates, not actual costs. If the estimates are higher than actual costs, a credit balance remains in the factory overhead control account.

31. (D) The first step under the weighted average method is to determine the units completed during the period. Then calculate the percentage complete using the ending inventory units. Adding those two numbers together equals equivalent units. The second step is to determine cost per (equivalent) unit.

32. (C) The question asks how many units would be included in the calculation of cost per equivalent unit under the weighted average method. To calculate cost per equivalent unit using the weighted average method, start with units completed for the period and then add the units still in ending inventory multiplied by the percent that they are complete.

Units completed during the period	400
Ending inventory units × 75 percent complete (200 × 0.75)	+150
Equivalent units in ending inventory	550

33. (B) To calculate cost per equivalent unit using the weighted average method, the numerator includes both current costs and beginning inventory costs as follows:

$650,000 current costs + $32,000 beginning inventory costs = $682,000

34. (A) The cost per equivalent unit of material production is calculated as follows:

$682,000 ÷ 550 units = $1,240

To calculate cost per equivalent unit using the weighted average method, the numerator includes both current costs and beginning inventory costs as follows:

Current costs	$650,000
Beginning inventory costs	+ $32,000
	$682,000

To calculate cost per equivalent unit using weighted average, the denominator starts with units completed for the period and then adds the ending inventory units times the percent complete.

Units completed during the period	400
Ending inventory units, 75 percent complete (200 × 0.75)	+ 150
Equivalent units in ending inventory	550

35. (B) Under the FIFO method, 500 equivalent units are calculated as follows: To calculate cost per equivalent unit using FIFO, start with beginning inventory units:

100 units, 50 percent complete (100 × 0.50)	50 units
Units completed for the period	+ 400 units
Beginning inventory	− 100 units
Subtotal	350 units
Ending inventory units × the percent complete (200 × 0.75)	+ 150 units
Equivalent units	500 units

36. (C) To calculate cost per equivalent unit using FIFO, the numerator includes current costs only: current costs $650,000.

37. (B) To calculate cost per equivalent unit using FIFO, the first step is to calculate the equivalent units for the period (denominator). Using the FIFO method, 500 equivalent units are calculated as follows:

Beginning inventory units (50% complete, 100 units work this period)	50 units
Units completed for the period	+ 400 units
Beginning inventory	− 100 units
Subtotal	350 units
Ending inventory units × the percent complete (200 units × 0.75)	+ 150 units
Equivalent units using FIFO	500 units

In determining costs per equivalent unit, the second step is to calculate the numerator, or total costs. To calculate cost per equivalent unit using FIFO, the numerator includes current costs only, or $650,000. To calculate cost per equivalent unit using FIFO, the final step is to divide costs by equivalent units calculated.

$650,000 total costs ÷ 500 units = $1,300 cost per equivalent unit

38. (C) I and II are correct. To calculate equivalent cost per unit using weighted average, use both current costs and beginning inventory cost in the numerator and divide by the number of equivalent units.

39. (B) II is correct. Regardless of the method used, the formula for cost per equivalent unit is total costs divided by number of equivalent units. Using FIFO, the number of equivalent units (denominator) includes beginning inventory units. I is wrong. Using weighted average, the starting point for the calculation of number of equivalent units (denominator) is the number of units completed and transferred out during the period. Using weighted average, the beginning inventory units are not considered in the calculation of equivalent units.

40. (A) I is correct. To calculate cost per equivalent unit using FIFO, use only current costs in the numerator. II is wrong. To calculate cost per equivalent unit using FIFO, use current costs, *not* beginning inventory costs, in the numerator.

41. (C) I and II are correct. When calculating equivalent units, treatment of ending inventory by the FIFO and weighted average methods is identical.

42. (B) II is correct. Using process costing, FIFO considers beginning inventory units (in the denominator) but not beginning inventory costs (in the numerator) when determining cost per equivalent unit. I is wrong. Weighted average does not consider beginning inventory units (in the denominator) when calculating cost per equivalent unit, but weighted average does consider beginning inventory costs (in the numerator).

43. (C) Activity-based costing describes a system that accumulates all costs of overhead for each of the departments or activities of the organization and then allocates those overhead costs based on causal factors, factors that caused the department or activity to incur overhead. Conversely, traditional costing allocates overhead for all departments of an organization by use of a single company-wide overhead allocation rate. For this reason, activity-based costing is considered a more sophisticated and accurate method of applying overhead than traditional costing methods. (A) is wrong. Process costing is a method of allocating production costs to products and services by averaging the costs over the total units produced. (B) is wrong. Job-order costing is a method of allocating production costs to products and services that are identifiable as separate units, custom-made goods that require different amounts of labor and materials to complete.

44. (A) I and II are correct. By using more than one cost driver, activity-based costing provides management with a more thorough understanding of product costs and product profitability. In addition, activity-based costing leads to a more competitive position by evaluating cost drivers. In activity-based costing, cost reduction is accomplished by identifying and eliminating nonvalue-adding activities. Reducing and eliminating nonvalue-adding activities will lower overall cost. III is wrong. The benefit that management can expect from traditional costing (not activity-based costing) includes using a common departmental or factory-wide measure of activity, such as direct labor hours or dollars, to distribute manufacturing overhead to products.

45. (C) I and II are correct. Eliminating nonvalue-adding activities would reduce costs, which is one of the objectives of activity-based costing systems. Eliminating all cost drivers would eliminate all activity. Since most activities add value, management would only want to eliminate nonvalue-added activities. Value-added activities have their costs, but they are necessary, as they add value.

46. (D) II is correct. Process costing is a method of allocating production costs to products and services by averaging the cost over the total units produced. Costs are usually accumulated by department rather than by job. I is wrong. Job-order costing accumulates costs per job. III is wrong. Activity-based costing allocates overhead on the basis of multiple cost drivers, rather than just a single cost driver.

47. (B) I and II are correct. Activity-based costing involves using cost drivers as application bases to increase the accuracy of reported product costs. In addition, activity-based costing involves using several machine cost pools to measure product costs on the basis of time in a machine center. III is wrong. Plant-wide application rates applied to machine hours is a traditional costing approach, not an activity-based costing approach. Activity-based costing involves the more detailed and accurate cost allocations that are now preferred in manufacturing.

48. (A) I is correct. Activity-based costing uses cause-and-effect relationships to capitalize costs to inventory. This is not acceptable for external reporting but useful to management for internal reporting. II is wrong. Job-order costing (a simple accumulation of costs associated with a specific job) is acceptable for both internal and external purposes. III is wrong. Process costing is acceptable for both internal and external purposes. Process costing involves an averaging of actual costs.

49. (C) I and II are correct. The difference between variable and absorption costing is the manner in which fixed manufacturing costs are treated. Using variable costing, only variable costs are included in inventory. Consequently, the difference in net income using variable costing versus absorption costing is the amount of fixed manufacturing costs (accounted for in inventory using absorption costing) multiplied by the change in inventory. An increase in inventory indicates that a portion of the fixed costs associated with inventory using absorption costing is expensed using variable costing. Absorption costing, therefore, produces greater income than variable costing, as inventory levels increase as follows:

Change in inventory (increase)	2,000 units
Fixed manufacturing cost per unit (absorbed into inventory, excluded from cost of goods sold)	$40
Higher net income using absorption costing	$80,000

50. (B) I and III are correct. Other terms for the contribution approach are *direct costing* and *variable costing*. II is wrong. Full absorption costing is the opposite of the contribution approach. The direct, or variable, costing or contribution margin approach excludes fixed costs from product (inventoried) costs. Full absorption costing includes those fixed costs in ending inventory.

51. (A) I is correct. Direct (sometimes called variable) costing can be used for internal purposes only; GAAP prefers absorption costing. II is wrong. Direct costing is not used for the benefit of external users. Variable costs exclude fixed costs from product (inventoried) costs and thereby produce an income statement based on contribution margin, highly useful to internal managers in computing breakeven points and analyzing performance but not useful for external reporting.

52. (B) II is correct. Using absorption costing, costs are broken down between product and period.

53. (C) I and II are correct. Using variable costing, all fixed factory overhead is treated as a period cost and is expensed in the period incurred. The cost of inventory includes only variable manufacturing costs. Using variable costing, the cost of goods sold includes only variable costs. Also, the variable selling, general, and administrative expenses are part of total variable costs.

54. (C) I and II are correct. Fixed selling, general, and administrative costs are always period costs whether direct costing or full absorption costing is used. Using variable costing, all fixed factory overhead is treated as a period cost and is expensed in the period incurred. The cost of inventory includes only variable manufacturing costs, so the cost of goods sold includes only variable costs. Also, the variable selling, general, and administrative expenses are part of total variable costs.

55. (C) The difference between variable costing and full absorption costing is the treatment of fixed manufacturing costs. Full absorption costing treats fixed manufacturing costs as product costs, while variable costing expenses these as period costs.

56. (D) The difference between variable costing and full absorption costing is the treatment of fixed manufacturing costs. Full absorption costing treats fixed manufacturing costs as product costs, while variable costing expenses fixed manufacturing as period costs. Variable costing treats all fixed costs as period costs, expensing the costs regardless of sales.

57. (C) The difference between variable costing and full absorption costing is the treatment of fixed manufacturing costs. Full absorption costing treats fixed manufacturing costs as product costs, while variable costing expenses these as period costs. Using full absorption costing:

Fixed manufacturing costs $195,000 ÷ 100,000 units produced =
                                            $1.95 per unit produced
$1.95 fixed manufacturing costs per unit × 75,000 units sold = $146,250 fixed
    manufacturing costs expensed (through cost of goods sold) using full absorption
    costing

Using full absorption costing, the remaining fixed manufacturing costs of $48,750 ($195,000 − $146,250) remain in inventory as product costs.

58. (B) Variable costing treats all fixed costs as period costs and would expense $195,000 in the period incurred regardless of sales. Thus, the difference in net income would be the amount of fixed manufacturing costs inventoried using absorption costing ($195,000 − $146,250 = $48,750). Using full absorption costing:

Fixed manufacturing costs $195,000 ÷ 100,000 units produced =
                                            $1.95 per unit produced
$1.95 fixed manufacturing costs × 75,000 units sold = $146,250 fixed manufacturing
    costs expensed (through cost of goods sold) using full absorption costing

Using full absorption costing, the remaining fixed manufacturing costs of $48,750 ($195,000 − $146,250) remain in inventory as product costs.

59. (C) I and II are correct. When production exceeds sales, inventory increases. As inventory increases, net income using absorption costing benefits from fixed manufacturing overhead that is recorded in inventory instead of recognized in cost of goods sold. When sales exceed production, inventory falls. As inventory falls, net income using absorption costing is reduced by cost of goods sold that includes fixed manufacturing overhead from prior periods that had been recorded in inventory. As a result, when sales exceed production, absorption costing net income is less than variable costing net income.

60. (A) The ending finished goods inventory computed using direct costing is calculated by allocating the total costs capitalized in inventory using direct (variable) costing to ending inventory as follows:

Direct materials used	$180,000
Direct labor incurred	+ $140,000
Variable factory overhead	+ $124,000
Total production	$444,000

$444,000 ÷ 40,000 units produced = $11.10 per unit

$11.10 per unit × 3,000 units on hand = $33,300

61. (C) I and II are correct. Using variable costing, all fixed factory overhead is treated as a period cost and is expensed in the period incurred. The cost of inventory includes only variable manufacturing costs, so the cost of goods sold includes only variable costs.

62. (A) Contribution margin is calculated as sales less all variable costs, even variable selling, general, and administrative costs.

63. (C) I and II are correct. Contribution margin is calculated as sales less all variable costs. Cost of goods sold includes only *product costs* that are variable, not variable selling and general expenses. Variable selling and general expenses would be a period cost and not part of cost of goods sold, although they would be included in the calculation of contribution margin.

64. (A) I is correct. Contribution margin includes *all* variable costs, while cost of goods sold includes only product costs that are variable.

65. (B) The calculation of contribution margin is for internal purposes and includes sales less all variable costs.

66. (A) The contribution margin is calculated as follows:

Sales − Variable costs = Contribution margin

Sales	$750,000
Variable manufacturing costs	− $140,000
Variable selling and general costs	− $45,000
Contribution margin	$565,000

67. (A) Contribution margin can be calculated as selling price less all variable costs:

Sales	$160
Direct materials	− $20
Direct labor	− $15
Factory overhead	− $12
Shipping and handling	− $3
Variable cost per unit	$50
Contribution margin	$110

68. (C) Contribution margin can be calculated as selling price less all variable costs:

Sales	$160
Direct materials	− $20
Direct labor	− $15
Factory overhead	− $12
Shipping and handling	− $3
Variable cost per unit	$50
Gross sales ($160 per unit × 18,000 units)	$2,880,000
Sales returns and allowances	− $80,000
Net sales	$2,800,000
Variable costs	− $900,000*
Contribution margin	$1,900,000

69. (D) I and II are wrong. Variable costs vary in total with production and sales, but on a per unit basis, variable costs per unit do *not* change with production. Contribution margin is made up of variable costs (subtracted from sales). Since variable costs per unit do not change with production and sales, contribution margin per unit does not change with production and sales.

70. (A) The contribution margin is calculated as follows:

Sales	$750,000
Variable manufacturing costs	− $130,000
Variable selling and administrative costs	− $45,000
Contribution margin	$575,000

$575,000 ÷ 55,000 units = $10.45 contribution margin per unit

Note that variable costs per unit are assumed to remain unchanged from year to year.

71. (A) Four hundred units must be sold to break even. To find the breakeven point, divide the total fixed cost ($80,000) by the contribution margin per unit ($200).

72. (D) Breakeven analysis can be used to calculate the required sales dollars to break even using the following formula:

Sales = Fixed costs ÷ Contribution margin ratio (contribution margin expressed as a percentage of revenue)

---

*$900,000 = $50 variable costs per unit × $18,000 units

The fact pattern indicates that variable costs are 20 percent of sales. By extension, contribution must be 80 percent of sales (100% − 20%). The breakeven in sales dollars is computed using the formula based upon fixed costs given at $30,000:

$30,000 fixed costs ÷ 80% contribution margin = $37,500

73. **(B)** Fixed costs can be calculated as follows:

Selling price is given at $7.50.
Variable costs are given at $2.25.
Contribution margin is $5.25/unit.
Breakeven in units is given at 20,000.

Fixed costs can then be calculated as follows:

Fixed costs ÷ $5.25 = 20,000 units to break even
20,000 × $5.25 = $105,000

74. **(C)** Selling price per unit less variable cost per unit equals contribution margin per unit.

$9 − $3 variable costs = $6 contribution margin per unit

New variable cost is calculated by multiplying old variable cost by 1.333.

$2.25 × 1.333 = $3 variable cost per unit
$9 − $3 = $6

75. **(D)** Fixed costs were calculated for Year 1 at $105,000, so just multiply by 1.2; fixed costs for Year 2 are $126,000.

76. **(C)** Breakeven in units equals fixed costs divided by contribution margin per unit. Year 2 fixed costs were calculated in Question 75 at $126,000. Contribution margin per unit in Year 2 is $6.

$126,000 ÷ $6 = 21,000 units

77. **(C)** Total variable costs include:

Direct materials	$10
Direct labor	+ $7
Delivery charges	+ $5
Commission ($100 × 10%)	+ $10
Total variable costs per unit	$32

78. **(C)** Fixed costs include indirect factory costs and administrative costs, or $5,000 and $20,200 every month.

79. **(A)** The breakeven point in units (helmets) is computed as fixed costs divided by contribution margin per unit. Contribution margin is computed as the difference between selling price and variable costs. Variable costs include the following:

Direct materials	$10
Direct labor	+ $7

Delivery charges	+ $5
Commission ($100 × 10%)	+ $10
Total variable costs per unit	$32

Contribution margin = $100 sales price − $32 = $68

Fixed costs comprise the following:

Indirect factory costs	$5,000
Administrative costs	+ $20,200
Total fixed costs	$25,200

Breakeven point in units is computed as follows:

$25,200 fixed costs ÷ $68 contribution margin per unit =
371 helmets required to break even

80. **(C)** The number of units is calculated as follows:

$240,000 desired profit + $100,000 fixed cost = $340,000
$340,000 ÷ $200 contribution margin = 1,700 units required to earn desired profit

81. **(B)** The 12,500 units are calculated as follows:

Price	$20
Direct materials	− $3.25
Direct labor	− $4
Freight out	− $0.75
Total variable cost	$8
Contribution margin	$12
Fixed costs	$100,000
Pretax profit desired	+ $50,000
Total fixed costs	$150,000

$150,000 total fixed costs ÷ $12 contribution margin per unit = 12,500 units required to achieve $50,000 pretax profit.

82. **(B)** The pretax profit is calculated as follows:

Targeted profit before tax = targeted profit after tax ÷ 1 − tax rate
$100,000 ÷ 0.65 = $153,846

83. **(D)** The breakeven is calculated as follows:

Breakeven in sales dollars = $70,000 fixed costs ÷ contribution margin ratio
Breakeven in sales dollars = $70,000 ÷ ($120,000 ÷ $200,000) =
$70,000 ÷ 0.60 = $116,667 breakeven in sales dollars

84. **(D)** The margin of safety is the difference between current sales and breakeven in sales. Breakeven sales is calculated by dividing fixed costs by the contribution margin ratio:

Breakeven in sales = $70,000 fixed costs ÷ contribution margin ratio
Breakeven in sales = $70,000 ÷ ($120,000 ÷ $200,000)
$70,000 ÷ 0.60 = $116,667 breakeven in sales
$200,000 current sales − $116,667 breakeven in sales = $83,333 margin of safety

85. (B) II is correct. Breakeven analysis assumes that fixed costs in total are constant over a relevant range. I is wrong. While variable costs vary in total with production, breakeven analysis assumes that all variable costs and revenues are constant on a per unit basis.

86. (C) I and II are correct. Breakeven analysis assumes that all variable costs and revenues are constant on a per unit basis and linear over a relevant range.

87. (C) When considering a special order, a manufacturer would accept the special order if the sales price were in excess of the relevant costs. Relevant costs differ depending upon whether the manufacturer is already at full capacity. If already at full capacity, the relevant costs include not just all variable costs but opportunity costs as well. If there is excess capacity in the factory, relevant costs include only variable costs.

88. (C) I and II are correct. At full capacity, relevant costs include variable costs and opportunity costs. Opportunity costs are the forfeited profits from product A that will be sacrificed in order to produce the special order.

89. (A) The minimum acceptable selling price should include only the incremental costs associated with the order: \$23,000 variable costs + \$8,750 external designers costs = \$31,750. Note that this is a special order (won't affect regular sales) and there is already idle capacity.

90. (C) I and II are correct. Using breakeven analysis, total variable costs are directly proportional to volume over a relevant range, and selling prices are to remain unchanged if breakeven analysis is to be utilized.

91. (B) Total fixed costs do not change and operating income increases. Adding a job with a positive contribution margin within idle capacity will increase operating income. The company will still make a profit for the special order even though the gross profit percent will be lower. The question states that fixed costs in total will be the same (fixed costs are assumed to be the same if the company is operating within the relevant range). Variable costs *per unit* will be the same. Note that fixed costs per unit decrease with increased production. (A) and (C) are wrong. Fixed costs will not change within the relevant range, and fixed cost per unit would decrease, not increase. (D) is wrong. Operating income will increase since the new job has a positive margin and is utilizing otherwise idle capacity.

92. (C) Opportunity cost is the potential benefit lost by selecting a particular course of action.

93. (C) I and II are correct. Opportunity cost is the potential benefit lost by selecting a particular course of action. If idle space has no alternative use, there is no benefit forgone; opportunity cost is zero. In addition, when deciding on special orders with no opportunity cost, the order would be accepted if the selling price per unit was higher than the variable cost per unit.

94. (B) II is correct. When deciding between make or buy, fixed costs should be ignored unless those fixed costs would be avoided by purchasing the product instead of making the product.

95. (D) The opportunity cost is the next best use of the productive capacity, not the total of the two or the difference between the two. Opportunity cost is the value of the road *not* traveled.

96. (C) The opportunity cost is $15,000, the value of the next best use of the space. The alternative selected carries a contribution margin of $20,000, and the next best use is renting the space for $15,000. The opportunity cost is *not* $35,000, the combined value of the alternative selected and the next best use. The opportunity cost is the next best use of the productive capacity ($15,000), not the difference between the best and next best alternatives ($20,000 − $15,000).

97. (A) I is correct. The relevance of a particular cost to a decision is determined by the potential effect that the cost has on the decision. Relevant costs are expected future costs that vary with the action taken. II is wrong. Whether a cost is relevant to a particular decision has nothing to do with the number of decision alternatives.

98. (C) I and II are correct. Avoidable costs would be relevant and so would incremental costs. Costs are relevant costs if they change with the decision to produce an additional amount of the unit over the present output.

99. (C) I and II are correct. The operational decision method, referred to as marginal analysis, is used when analyzing business decisions such as the introduction of a new product. Operational decision analysis is also used when analyzing business decisions such as acceptance or rejection of special orders, making versus buying a product or service, and adding or dropping a segment. Marginal analysis is also used in deciding whether to change output levels of existing products.

100. (D) I and II are wrong. Note that this is a NOT question. The operational decision method, referred to as marginal analysis, *is* used when analyzing business decisions such as acceptance or rejection of special orders and making versus buying a product or service.

101. (A) I is correct. Costs that change using different alternatives are known as relevant costs. The relevance of a particular cost to a decision is determined by its potential effect on the decision. Relevant costs are expected future costs that vary with the action taken. II is wrong. If the cost varies with production of the next unit, it is a relevant cost and should be considered by management.

102. (A) I is correct. Joint costs are sunk costs, incurred already, and are *not* relevant to the sell or process further decision. Joint costs occur when two (or more) main products start from the same process and then eventually become different identifiable products. All the costs up to the point that the products become identifiable are known as joint costs. The point where the two distinct products can be identified is known as the split-off point. II is wrong. Separable costs are the costs incurred after the split-off point. The sell or process further decision would need to take into consideration separable costs because separable costs may not need to be incurred if the identifiable product can be sold once the split-off point occurs. Conversely, if the identifiable product cannot be sold or cannot be sold for much money at the split-off point, then separable costs may need to be incurred to increase the value of the joint product.

103. (B) The question requires allocation based on quantity of units produced, as follows:

Total units Quo	30,000 units (30/90 = 1/3)
Rael	+ 60,000 units (60/90 = 2/3)
Total units	90,000

Allocation of joint costs:

Quo	$1/3 \times \$150{,}000 = \$50{,}000$
Rael	$2/3 \times \$150{,}000 = \$100{,}000$

Notice that the selling price per unit was not needed because the joint cost allocation was to be based on physical quantity only. There is another method of allocating joint costs based on relative selling price. (See answer to Question 104.)

104. (D) The joint cost to be allocated to Rael is calculated as follows:

Quo	30,000 units $\times$ \$3 = \$90,000
Rael	60,000 units $\times$ \$6 = \$360,000
Quo	$\$90{,}000 \div \$450{,}000 = 20\%$
Rael	$\$360{,}000 \div \$450{,}000 = 80\%$
Joint costs allocated to Quo	$20\% \times \$150{,}000 = \$30{,}000$
Joint costs allocated to Rael	$80\% \times \$150{,}000 = \$120{,}000$

105. (C) The joint cost to be allocated is calculated as follows:

30,000 units of product A + 20,000 units of product B = 50,000 total units

A physical quantity allocation basis ignores selling price at the split-off point and just prorates based on physical quantity. Therefore, 30,000 units of product A divided by 50,000 units equals 60%.

60% $\times$ \$400,000 of joint cost = \$240,000 of joint cost allocated to product A

106. (C) I and II are correct. Incremental costs are relevant costs. Incremental costs are relevant because they include costs that vary with the decision to produce an additional amount of the unit over the present output. Prime costs (direct materials and direct labor) are incremental costs and would be relevant because they too vary with the decision to produce an additional amount of the unit over the present output.

107. (D) The decision to drop a segment is based on a comparison of cost and benefit. The benefit of dropping the segment is the avoidable fixed costs associated with ejecting the segment. The benefit of avoidable fixed costs is compared with the contribution margin lost.

108. (B) A regression equation estimates the dependent variable based on changes in the independent variable.

109. (B) The correlation coefficient measures the strength of the relationship between the dependent variable and the independent variable. The correlation coefficient is always a number between -1 and $+1$. If the relationship is strong, it will have a coefficient near $+1$ or -1, depending on the slope of the relationship. (D) is wrong. Linear regression analysis is a statistical method that fits a line to the data by the least squares method. It is the most accurate way to classify costs of an object as either fixed or variable.

110. (B) The total cost formula is the formula where total cost, the dependent variable (y), is equal to volume times the independent variable (variable costs [x]) plus a constant (fixed costs).

111. (A) The total cost formula is the formula for a line where total cost, the dependent variable (y), is equal to volume times the independent variable (variable costs [x]) plus a constant (fixed costs).

112. (A) The correlation coefficient is always a number between -1 and $+1$. If the relationship is strong, it will have a coefficient near $+1$ or -1, depending on the slope of the relationship. Change in total cost is almost totally dependent on volume; therefore, the relationship between the two will be a positive number close to 1.0. As volume goes up, total cost goes up; the slope is positive. (C) is wrong. A correlation coefficient of zero would indicate no relationship between volume and total cost.

113. (B) II is correct. The coefficient of determination measures the total variation in "y"—or total cost—that is explained by the total variation in the independent variable, x, or variable costs. I is wrong. The plan is to produce 150 units, so total cost, y, is computed as follows:

$y = \$80$ variable cost per unit $\times$ 150 units $= \$12,000 + \$25$ fixed costs $= \$12,025$

114. (A) I is correct. Cost volume relationships are not only positive but also assumed to be proportional since total cost increases with volume. II is wrong. A coefficient of correlation of zero indicates no relationship between costs and volume. We would expect this relationship for fixed costs, not variable costs.

115. (C) Management will choose a cost driver or independent variable based on a number close to 1.0 or even -1.0. This would indicate that a lot of the change in the dependent variable is determined by the independent variable, and that would be considered a good regression model, full of useful information. On the other hand, if the coefficient of correlation is zero or close to zero, there is little or no relationship between the dependent variable and the independent variable, so that cost driver would be *least* likely chosen.

116. (D) I and II are correct. When choosing independent variables like cost drivers, management would choose the cost driver with the highest coefficient of correlation, either positive or negative. III is wrong. If the coefficient of correlation is zero or close to zero, there is little or no relationship between the dependent variable and the independent variable, so that cost driver would be *least* likely chosen.

117. (D) I and II are wrong. The high-low method is a simplified approach to classifying costs as fixed and variable. The high-low method uses only the points of highest and lowest activity. Regression analysis is a statistical method that is the most accurate way to classify costs of an object as either fixed or variable because the regression method considers every point of activity, not just the highest and lowest points.

118. (B) The calculation for the high-low method is as follows:

Volume ($520 - 364$)	156 units
Dollars ($\$8,350 - \$6,834$)	$\$1,516$

Using the high-low method, the variable cost per unit is equal to the change in dependent variable divided by the change in independent variable, or $\$1,516 \div 156 = \$9.72$ variable cost per unit. Therefore, $\$9.72$ of cost is added for each additional unit produced.

119. (B) Since variable costs are $9.72 per unit, $9.72 times 520 units produced in December equals $5,054 variable costs for December. Since total costs for December were $8,350, just subtract variable costs for December of $5,054, and fixed costs for December must have been $3,296.

Chapter 2: Planning and Budgeting

120. (A) I and II are correct. Participative budgeting allows for increased motivation because it seeks input from multiple parties and spreads the decision-making process over multiple layers of managers and individuals. Implementing participative budgeting is also more time consuming because it requires input from multiple parties and spreads the decision-making process over multiple layers of managers and individuals. III is wrong. Implementing participative budgeting is more time consuming but allows for wider acceptance because more people are involved.

121. (D) I and II are wrong. Note that this question asks what would *not* be contained in the master budget. The annual business plan, the master budget, includes operating budgets. The operating budget process includes all budgets except cash and capital purchases budgets. The operating budget also includes the pro forma income statement. The annual business plan also includes financial budgets. The financial budget process includes cash and capital purchases budgets, the balance sheet, and the statement of cash flows. With both operating budgets and financial budgets, the annual business plan is prepared in anticipation of achieving a single level of sales volume for a specific period.

122. (A) I is correct. The operating budget process includes the pro forma income statement and all budgets except the cash budget and capital purchases. II is wrong. The financial budget process includes cash and capital purchases budgets, the budgeted balance sheet, and the statement of cash flows.

123. (D) I and II are wrong. The budgeting process usually begins with the sales budget, then the production budget, and toward the end of the budgeting process, the cash budget is prepared.

124. (B) II is correct. When preparing a budget, the last budget to be prepared is the cash budget. Pro forma accrual financial statements are prepared after the cash budget. I is wrong. The sales budget is the first budget prepared.

125. (D) The capital expenditures budget is developed independently but must take into account the cash available. The production budget is based on the sales budget, with adjustments for any changes in planned inventory levels.

126. (C) I and II are correct. A flexible budget provides cost allowances (adjustments) for different levels of activity. A static budget provides fixed and variable costs for one level of activity. Both flexible and static budgets include both variable and fixed costs and, therefore, are appropriate for planning purposes. While the question didn't ask this, a flexible budget is better than a static budget for evaluating performance since it can be adjusted to the actual production level.

127. (A) I is correct. A static budget is based on costs at one level of output. Static budgets include budgeted costs for budgeted, not actual, output. II is wrong. Static budgets are not based on or adjusted for actual performance.

128. (D) The annual business plan process typically begins with operating budgets that are driven by sales budgets that, in turn, provide the required variables for production and personnel budgets. After those budgets are prepared, then the financial budgets can be prepared, including the cash budget.

129. (A) The order of budget preparation begins with the sales budget, which leads to the production budget (to support sales), which, in turn, leads to the direct material purchases budget (to support production), from which the cash disbursements budget is derived.

130. (B) I, II, and III are correct. Sales budgets are based upon sales forecasts, which are based on multiple independent variables like opinions of sales staff, past patterns of sales, general economic conditions, changes in the firm's prices, results of market research studies, and advertising and sales promotions.

131. (B) The calculation is as follows:

Budgeted sales	2,000 units
Ending inventory	+ 220 units
Beginning inventory	− 185 units
Desired level of production	2,035 units

Ignore prior-year beginning inventory.

132. (D) A 4 percent inflation rate would impact salary, health care costs, and rent expense. The budget would be computed as follows:

Salary expense ($210,000 × 1.04)	$218,400
Insurance expense ($120,000 × 1.04)	+ $124,800
Supplies expense ($60,000 × 1.04)	+ $62,400
Total budget for select items	$405,600

133. (D) A 4 percent inflation rate would impact salary, health care costs, and rent expense. The budget would be computed as follows:

Salary expense ($210,000 × 1.04)	$218,400
Insurance expense ($120,000 × 1.04)	+ $124,800
Supplies expense ($60,000 × 1.04)	+ $62,400
Depreciation expense ($25,000 × 1.0)	+ $25,000
Interest expense on 10-year fixed rate bonds	+ $27,000
Total budget for select items	$457,600

The depreciation and interest expense on fixed rate bonds would not be affected by inflation.

134. (B) Rascal should anticipate purchasing 820,000 wheels in July. Rascal would purchase enough wheels for 100,000 toy trucks planned for production as adjusted for 5,000 already on hand in anticipation of July production plus 7,500 purchased in anticipation of August production as follows:

July production (trucks)	100,000
Beginning inventory (5% × 100,000)	− 5,000
Ending inventory (5% × 150,000)	+ 7,500
Total trucks produced	102,500
Wheels per truck	× 8
Total purchases of wheels	820,000

135. (B) As calculated below, 360,000 units would need to be manufactured during Year 4 to support sales of 380,000 units:

Projected sales (units)	380,000
Desired ending inventory	+ 40,000
Required units	420,000
Beginning inventory	− 60,000
Required units to manufacture	360,000

136. (B) Production needs to cover the current budgeted sales for the current quarter while also taking into account desired inventory levels, as shown:

Second quarter sales	9,000
Desired ending inventory (10% × 12,000)	+ 1,200
Total units required	10,200
Beginning inventory (10% × 9,000)	− 900
Budgeted production	9,300 units

137. (D) In Year 1, 2,730 tables are to be produced during November, calculated as follows:

Budgeted sales for November	3,000
Desired ending inventory, Nov. 30 (30% × 2,100 Dec. sales)	+ 630
Total required	3,630
Beginning inventory, Nov. 1 (30% × 3,000 Nov. sales)	− 900
Production	2,730

138. (C) The $202,000 budgeted direct labor dollars for March is calculated as follows:

8,000 units × 3.0 hours × $6.75 = $162,000
8,000 units × 0.5 hour × $10 = $40,000

Total budgeted direct labor dollars for March $202,000

139. (C) I and II are correct. Overhead applied and material usage are inputs to the cost of goods manufactured. Direct labor is another input in cost of goods manufactured.

140. (B) II is correct. Work-in-process inventory affects both inputs (for beginning work in process) and outputs (for ending work in process). I is wrong. Finished goods inventory is not necessary for determining cost of goods manufactured but is necessary for calculating cost of goods sold. The calculation of a cost of goods manufactured budget includes materials, labor, and overhead applied.

141. (B) II is correct. The selling and administrative expense budget is dependent upon sales. I is wrong. The selling and administrative expense budget is operational, not financial. The selling and administrative expense budget represents the fixed and variable nonmanufacturing expenses anticipated during the budget period.

142. (B) Purchases in Year 1 should be budgeted to cover both the planned sales (cost = $200,000) and the desired increase in inventory ($13,000), for a total of $213,000. Accounts payable at Jan. 1, Year 1, will be paid in Year 1. Accounts payable at Dec. 31, Year 1, of $17,750 ($213,000 ÷ 12) will not be paid until Year 2. The total for Year 2 is calculated as follows:

Purchases	$213,000
Accounts payable paid in Year 1	+ $20,000
December purchase	− $17,750
Paid in Year 2	$215,250

143. (C) I and II are correct. The cash budget shows itemized cash receipts and disbursements during the period, including the financing activities and the beginning and ending cash balances. The main reason for preparing a cash budget is to anticipate cash flows so that excess cash can be invested and also to minimize the need for interim financing.

144. (A) I is correct. The cash budget helps to show the availability of funds for repayment of debt. II is wrong. The cash budget is usually broken down into monthly periods.

145. (B) The cash receipts can be calculated as follows:

October sales ($200,000 × 26%)	$52,000
November sales ($211,000 × 70%)	+ $147,700
Budgeted accounts receivable for December	$199,700

146. (A) I is correct. Borrowing funds on a note in August Year 4 would be a cash inflow in Year 4 and would have to be included in a schedule of cash receipts and disbursements for Year 4. The repayment would be a cash outflow in Year 5. II is wrong. Dividends declared are a noncash item until paid in Year 5.

147. (C) I and II are correct. A purchase order is a commitment but not a cash event. Uncollectible accounts are a noncash item.

148. (A) Cash collections for the second quarter comprise second quarter cash sales and collections of first quarter credit sales:

Second quarter cash sales (15,000 units × $4 × 70%)	$42,000
Collections of first quarter credit sales (10,000 units × $4 × 30%)	+ $12,000
Second quarter cash collections	$54,000

149. (B) The pro forma income statement is the first budgeted financial statement prepared. The budgeted income statement produces (anticipated) accrual basis net income or loss and is added to beginning owners' equity to generate the owners' equity section of the budgeted balance sheet. The budgeted statement of cash flows is usually the last pro forma financial statement prepared because so many things affect cash. Cash flow cannot be projected until everything else has been estimated.

150. (C) I and II are correct. The limitation of flexible budgeting is that flexible budgeting is highly dependent on an accurate identification of fixed cost and the variable cost per unit within the relevant range. The benefit of flexible budgeting is that, given the actual output, management can budget what revenue and expenses will be.

151. (C) I and II are correct. Planned additions of capital equipment and related debt from the capital budget are added to the pro forma balance sheet. Planned financing expenses and principal repayments on capital equipment additions are included as disbursements on the cash budget.

152. (D) A flexible budget is a budget prepared at different levels of operating activity. It is appropriate for all industries and any activity that has variable costs and direct labor.

153. (D) I, II, and III are correct. The selling price per unit, the variable cost per unit, and the total fixed cost remain constant regardless of volume within the relevant range. Since the selling price and variable costs remain constant, the contribution margin per unit will also remain the same regardless of volume within the relevant range. Flexible budgeting answers the question: What should revenue and expenses be, given an output change from the master budget? When starting with a master budget, the flexible number of units must be multiplied by the selling price per unit, the variable cost per unit, and the contribution margin per unit in order to convert from the master budget to the flexible budget.

154. (C) A master budget is an overall budget, consisting of many smaller budgets, that is based on one specific level of production. A flexible budget is a series of budgets based on different activity levels within the relevant range. A flexible budget contains budgeted costs for actual output.

155. (A) Contribution margin per unit equals $40,000 divided by 10,000 units, or $4 per unit. Flexible budgeting begins with a master budget, a static budget. Flexible budgeting converts from the master budget, the selling price per unit, the variable cost per unit, and the contribution margin per unit times the flexible number of units because the selling price per unit, the variable cost per unit, and the contribution margin per unit remain the same regardless of volume within the relevant range.

156. (C) The operating income can be calculated as follows:

July units (12,000 units × $4/unit contribution margin)	$48,000
Fixed costs (from master budget)	− $25,000
Operating income for July per flexible budget	$23,000

The primary feature of flexible budgets is the ability to adjust to actual volume based on established relationships between revenue and variable costs from the master budget.

157. (B) Variable costs are $14,500 and the variance is $500 favorable. Start by calculating budgeted variable costs per unit: $18,000 divided by 600 units equals $30/unit. Then multiply $30 per unit variable costs by the 500 actual units sold to equal $15,000 total (flexible) budgeted variable costs. Then $15,000 less actual variable costs of $14,500 equals $500 net favorable difference. This $500 difference represents $500 fewer dollars spent on variable costs than budgeted, which represents a favorable variance.

158. (B) The fixed cost variance is calculated as follows:

Actual fixed costs	$8,100
Budgeted fixed costs	− $8,800
Variance	$700 (favorable since actual fixed cost is less than budget)

159. (C) The flexible budget variance represents the difference between actual performance and the budget at the achieved volume. To calculate the variance, actual costs of $89,000 are compared to the flexible budget at actual volume levels, 9,000 units. Flexible budget is calculated by taking variable cost per unit from the original master budget of $10 per unit (given) and multiplying that by the actual level of volume, 9,000 units, equals $90,000. Therefore, $90,000 is the flexible budget variable cost. Actual costs incurred of $89,000 are compared to the forecasted costs of $90,000, which results in a $1,000 favorable flexible budget variance. The variance is favorable because actual expenses are less than the computed (flexible) budget.

160. (B) II is correct. Selling prices of finished goods depend on market prices of competitors, not costs. I is wrong. Identifying manufacturing variances and assigning their responsibility to a person or department does promote learning and improvement of operations through cost control measures.

161. (C) The price variance must be favorable because the actual cost is less than the standard cost, calculated as follows:

Price variance = (Standard price − Actual price) × Actual units
Price variance = ($30 standard − $28.50 actual) × 11,400 actual units needed
Price variance = $1.50 × 11,400 = $17,100 favorable

162. (D) Imhoff Company experienced an unfavorable direct materials price variance for the current period. The materials price variance formula is calculated as follows:

Materials price variance = Actual quantity × (Actual price − Standard price)
Materials price variance = 15,000 × ($9.50 − $7)
Materials price variance = 15,000 × $2.50 = ($37,500) unfavorable

163. (D) The difference between the standard hours at standard wage rates and actual hours at standard wage rates is referred to as the direct labor efficiency variance or labor usage variance.

164. (D) Material Tyrisis experienced a favorable direct materials price variance for the current period. The materials price variance formula is calculated as follows:

Materials price variance = Actual quantity × (Actual price − Standard price)
Materials price variance = 3,500 × ($4.80 − $5)
Materials price variance = $700 favorable

The materials price variance is favorable since less money was actually spent than the standard.

165. (C) I and II are correct. An unfavorable direct labor efficiency variance could be caused by an unfavorable material usage variance. Poor quality materials could mean unfavorable material usage and cause inefficient labor usage. In addition, the actual hours at the standard rate compared to the standard hours at the standard rate is referred to as the direct labor efficiency variance.

166. (B) II is correct. Inadequate supervision pertains to management of employees and materials and results in usage variances. I is wrong. Price variances would not be caused by inadequate supervision but rather by purchasing from suppliers other than those offering the most favorable terms, purchasing nonstandard or uneconomical lots, and failing to correctly forecast price increases.

167. (A) The purchase of higher than standard quality material would likely result in an unfavorable material price variance (the better material costs more) and a favorable material usage variance (the better material causes less waste).

168. (B) The direct labor price variance is calculated as follows:

Actual labor price = $840,000 ÷ 84,000 hours = $10/hour
Standard labor price   − $9/hour
Variance per hour $1/hour unfavorable
Direct labor hours worked × 84,000
Direct labor price variance $84,000 unfavorable

169. (A) It is an unfavorable direct labor efficiency variance:

Actual direct labor hours worked   84,000
Standard direct labor hours
(20,000 actual generators × 4 standard hours)   − 80,000
Excess labor hours   4,000
$9 standard labor rate × 4,000 excess hours = ($36,000) unfavorable direct labor
    efficiency variance

The variance is unfavorable since more hours were worked than budgeted.

170. (D) The variance can be calculated as follows:

Standard price $1.70
Actual price   − $1.85
Difference $0.15 unfavorable since more was paid than the standard
$0.15 × 59 lbs. actual quantity purchased × 1,750 actual units produced =
    $15,488 unfavorable

171. (C) The variance can be calculated as follows:

Standard labor rate $12 per hour
Actual labor rate $12.50 per hour
Difference of $0.50 per hour unfavorable
0.5 hour × 3.5 hours per unit × 1,750 actual units = $3,063 variance, unfavorable
    since Barlow paid more for labor than the standard amount

172. (C) Overhead is being applied based on a cost driver of $9 per direct labor hour. The overhead efficiency variance compares the amount of the variable overhead applied using standard rates to the amount of variable overhead that would have been applied at actual. If more was applied than would have been incurred, the results are favorable.

Standard hours allowed	11,000
Application rate	× $9
Total standard hours cost	$99,000
Actual hours	10,000
Application rate	× $9
Total actual hours cost	$90,000
	9,000 favorable overhead efficiency variance

173. (B) Selling price variance is the actual selling price less the budgeted selling price times the actual number of units.

$16 actual selling price − $13 budgeted selling price = $3 favorable selling price
$3 × 4,000 actual units sold = $12,000 favorable selling price variance

174. (A) Harper Company's variable overhead spending variance is $200 favorable. Both variable overhead rates are multiplied by the actual cost driver of 50 process hours. The actual overhead rate of $16 times the cost driver of 50 hours equals $800. Next, the standard overhead rate of $20 is multiplied by the actual cost driver of 50 hours to equal $1,000. The actual amount charged to the overhead account ($800) is less than the amount applied ($1,000), so the $200 variance is favorable.

175. (B) II is correct. Sales volume variance arises when the quantity budgeted to be sold differs from the quantity sold. I is wrong. The sales price variance is based on the actual number of units sold and does not take into account the number of units budgeted to be sold.

176. (D) The direct materials price variance could be used to monitor the purchasing manager's performance. (A) and (C) are wrong. The materials usage variance relates to the amount of materials used and would be influenced most significantly by the production manager, not the purchasing manager. (B) is wrong. The direct labor rate variance is influenced not by the purchasing manager but by the human resources department.

177. (C) I and II are correct. The balanced scorecard seeks to fully integrate financial measures of performance with nonfinancial measures of performance. It demonstrates that no single dimension of organizational performance can be relied upon to evaluate success. These critical success factors are often classified as human resources, business process, customer satisfaction, and financial performance.

178. (D) I, II, and III are correct. Cost centers are responsible for costs only. Profit centers are responsible for revenues and expenses. Investment centers are responsible for revenues, expenses, and invested capital. Responsibility accounting is a system of accounting that recognizes various responsibility or decision centers throughout an organization and reflects the plans and actions of each of these centers by assigning particular revenues and costs to the one having the responsibility for making decisions about those revenues and costs.

179. (C) From least to greatest responsibility, the correct order is cost, revenue, profit, and investment capital. Managers in a cost SBU only have responsibility to cut costs, and that is just one dimension of financial performance. Profit SBUs represent a greater responsibility than either cost or revenue SBUs. Profit SBUs require the manager to maintain control of revenues, costs, *and* the relationship between the two. Investment SBUs represent the highest level of responsibility. Managers consider not only cost, revenues, and their relationship, but also the relationship between assets invested and profits generated.

180. (D) The balanced scorecard demonstrates that no single dimension of organizational performance can be relied upon to evaluate success. The critical success factors are often classified as human resources, business process, customer satisfaction, and financial performance.

181. (D) I and II are correct. Responsibility accounting defines a profit center as being responsible for both revenues and costs. III is wrong. An investment center is responsible for revenues, costs, and invested capital.

182. (C) I and II are correct. An investment center is most like an independent business because investment centers are responsible for revenues, expenses, and invested capital.

183. (A) A performance report shows the budgeted and actual amounts and the variances between these amounts of key financial results appropriate for the type of responsibility center involved. I is correct. Controllable costs, as well as noncontrollable costs, are contained in a performance report for a cost center. II is wrong. Cost centers do not generate revenues and, therefore, would not have any revenues to include in a performance report.

184. (A) I is correct. The financial perspective of a balanced scorecard is concerned with the capture of increased market share. II is wrong. The learning and growth (advanced learning and innovation) perspective of a balanced scorecard is concerned with employee satisfaction and retention measures. The balanced scorecard demonstrates that no single dimension of organizational performance can be relied upon to evaluate success; thus, having financial and nonfinancial success factors makes it a "balanced" scorecard.

185. (A) I is correct. The "internal business" perspective of the balanced scorecard measures results of business operations by improvements in measures of efficiency. II is wrong. Employee satisfaction and retention measures are measured using the "learning and growth" perspective of the balanced scorecard. Employee satisfaction typically correlates with productivity, employee effectiveness, and retention.

186. (A) II is correct. Measures of financial performance would focus on results of operations and utilization of assets. I is wrong. The customer section of the balanced scorecard would focus on the company's defining its value in the marketplace. III is wrong. Learning and innovation would focus more on the effective use of personnel in improving business processes and linking rewards with recognition.

187. (B) Controllable margin is computed as contribution margin net of controllable costs. Controllable costs represent those fixed costs that managers can impact in less than one year.

188. (C) I and II are correct. Controllable margins are specifically defined as contribution margin less controllable fixed costs, and the reporting objective of controllable margin is to clearly define those margins for which a manager is responsible.

Chapter 3: Financial Management

189. (B) I, II, and III are correct. Differential and incremental costs represent the change in costs associated with two separate courses of action and are considered relevant. Avoidable costs represent the costs that can be averted by selecting different courses of action and are also considered relevant.

190. (C) III is correct. Sunk costs are unavoidable regardless of whatever alternative is ultimately selected. Since they have already been incurred, sunk costs are not relevant. I is wrong. Discretionary costs arise from periodic budgeting decisions; a company's decision to spend more on research and development is discretionary. Discretionary costs can change, so they are relevant. II is wrong. Opportunity costs are associated with forgoing the next best alternative when making a business decision; therefore, opportunity costs are relevant.

191. (B) II and III are correct. In decision analysis, financial factors and nonfinancial factors are relevant. Relevant nonfinancial factors would include employee morale that could lead to a loss of productivity. Opportunity costs are also relevant in decision analysis. I is wrong. In a decision analysis situation, relevant costs include avoidable (not unavoidable) costs.

192. (C) The $111,000 net cash outflow at the beginning of the first year is calculated as follows:

Purchase price	$100,000
Transportation cost	+ $7,000
Installation cost	+ $4,000
Net cash outflow at the beginning of the first year	$111,000

193. (A) The depreciation can be calculated as follows:

Purchase price	$100,000
Transportation cost	+ $7,000
Installation cost	+ $4,000
Net cash outflow at the beginning of the first year	$111,000
$111,000 ÷ 7 years = $15,857	

Notice that the asset was depreciated using 7 years rather than 10 years. In capital budgeting decisions, tax depreciation rather than book depreciation is considered relevant because tax depreciation reduces the taxable income, thereby reducing the cash payments for taxes.

194. (B) The net cash flow can be calculated as follows:

Cash inflow from selling (3,000 units × $300 per unit)	$900,000
Cash outflow for materials and labor	
(3,000 units × $250 per unit)	− $750,000
Cash inflow from operations	$150,000
Depreciation expense ($111,000 ÷ 7 years)	− $15,857
Taxable income	$134,143
Tax rate	× 30%
Tax to be paid	$40,243
Net cash flow in Year 2 after taxes ($150,000 − $40,243)	$109,757

195. (B) The net cash flow for Year 10 can be calculated as follows:

Cash inflow from selling (3,000 units × $300 per unit)	$900,000
Cash outflow for materials and labor (3,000 units × $250 per unit)	− $750,000
Cash inflow from operations	$150,000
Taxes paid at 30%	− $45,000
Cash inflow from operations after taxes	$105,000
Salvage value of equipment in Year 10	$4,000
Taxes paid at 30%	− $1,200
Cash inflow from sale of equipment after tax	+ $2,800
Total cash inflow after taxes ($105,000 + $2,800)	$107,800

The machine is fully depreciated in Year 10 because it was depreciated over a seven-year life. The tax basis of the machine is zero on the date Battaglia receives $4,000 salvage value for the machine. The gain on the machine of $4,000 ($4,000 salvage value − $0 basis) is taxed at 30 percent, or $1,200 in total tax outflow for the gain. The net inflows on the salvage is $2,800. Therefore, the total after-tax cash flows in Year 10 for the new machine would be $105,000 plus $2,800, or $107,800.

196. (A) III is correct. Note the question is asking for which is *not* part of net cash outflow. The tax savings from depreciation expense is not a net cash outflow. I and II are wrong. The net cash outflow does include the purchase price, transportation cost, and installation cost.

197. (B) The tax shield can be calculated as follows:

Cost of the asset	$90,000
Estimated life	÷ 10 years
Annual depreciation	$9,000
Annual depreciation tax shield ($9,000 × 0.3 tax rate)	$2,700

198. (C) I is correct. Net present value, like most capital budgeting techniques, focuses on cash flow. Cash flow is a pure measure of financial performance that limits the decision-making to the amount of cash the firm takes in and pays out for an investment. II is wrong. Net income distorts financial results with its noncash items, such as depreciation, as well as with sunk costs. III is wrong. Earnings before interest and taxes would distort financial results with noncash data (depreciation) as well as earnings data rather than the cash flow data most useful for capital budgeting.

199. (D) The original fair market value of the old equipment is a sunk cost that is irrelevant since it does not affect equipment replacement decisions. The items listed in II, III, and IV do affect the decision process.

200. (C) Opportunity cost is the potential benefit lost by selecting a particular course of action. If the land is developed rather than sold, giving up the potential selling price of the land is an opportunity cost. (A) is wrong. Sunk costs are those costs that have already been incurred, are unavoidable in the future, and are not relevant in the decision. (B) and (D) are wrong. Incremental costs and variable costs are costs of production that change in total as more units are produced.

201. (D) The original cost of the old machine, $40,000, is a sunk cost that will not change regardless of the decision that is made. Sunk costs are not relevant and would not be considered by Aron as part of the decision to keep or replace the current machine.

202. (B) I, II, and III are correct. The estimated salvage value of the old machine is relevant to the decision to keep or replace the machine. The salvage value will be realized if the machine is replaced but not realized if the machine is not replaced. The lower maintenance cost of the new machine is also relevant to the decision to keep or replace the old machine. The maintenance cost of the new machine will impact the comparative operating costs of the company and would be considered in the decision. Finally, the estimated salvage value and estimated useful life of the new machine would be relevant to the decision to keep or replace the old machine.

203. (D) The calculation is as follows:

Sales	$370,000
Variable costs	– $290,000
Cash inflows	$80,000
Tax rate 40%	– $32,000
Cash inflows net of tax	$48,000
Initial investment	$250,000
Useful life	10 years
Depreciation expense ($25,000 × 40%)	$10,000*

Cash inflows of $48,000 plus depreciation tax shield of $10,000 equals after-tax cash inflows of $58,000.

204. (C) I and III are correct. The decision to replace the old asset will result in the company paying the purchase price of the new asset, receiving the disposal price of the old asset, and recognizing a gain and paying taxes on the sale of the old asset based on cost less accumulated depreciation. II is wrong. Costs are deemed to be relevant if they change as a result of selecting different alternatives. The cost of the old asset will not change based on the decision to replace it. The cost of the old asset is a sunk cost and is not relevant to the decision on whether to replace it.

205. (A) The gain is calculated as follows:

Selling price	$13,300
Cost of the old asset less accumulated depreciation ($40,000 – $32,000)	– $8,000
Gain	$5,300
Multiplied by tax rate of 30%	= $1,590

With a tax rate of 30 percent, the additional taxes of $1,590 paid on the gain would be relevant to the decision whether to buy the new asset.

206. (A) I is correct. The annual net cash inflow includes the dollar amount of cash inflow times 1 minus the tax rate. II is wrong. Annual net cash inflow includes the depreciation expense times the tax rate. Although depreciation expense is not a cash expense, there is a cash inflow from depreciation. The depreciation expense on the tax return times the tax rate equals the annual depreciation tax shield, which is an additional cash inflow.

---

*Tax shield from noncash expense

207. (A) The net present value method of capital budgeting requires managers to evaluate the dollar amount of return rather than years to recover principal (payback method) or percentages of return (internal rate of return) as a means to screen investments. (B) is wrong. The internal rate of return focuses the decision maker on the discount rate at which the present value of the cash inflows equals the initial investment. (C) is wrong. The payback method takes the total investment in a project and divides it by its annual cash flows to determine the number of years it will take to gain a return of the initial investment.

208. (C) I and II are correct. Net present value is flexible and can be used when there is a different rate of return for each year of the project. If the cash inflows were not the same each year, the cash inflows would have to be multiplied by the present value of $1 (rather than the present value of an annuity). Although the net present value method does not provide the true rate of return on the investment, the net present value method indicates whether an investment will earn the hurdle rate of return. A positive net present value dollar amount indicates that the investment will earn the hurdle rate of return and the investment should be made. A negative net present value dollar amount indicates that the investment will *not* earn the hurdle rate and the project should be rejected.

209. (B) The net present value is calculated as follows:

Year	Cash Inflows		Present Value Factor		Net Present Value
1	$120,000	×	0.91	=	$109,200
2	$60,000	×	0.76	=	$45,600
3	$40,000	×	0.63	=	$25,200
4	$40,000	×	0.53	=	$21,200
5	$40,000	×	0.44	=	$17,600
Total					$218,800

$218,800 present value of cash inflows − $210,000 initial outlay = $8,800 net present value

The present value of $1 is used rather than the present value of an annuity because the annual cash flows are not the same.

210. (B) II is correct. If the present value of cash outflows is less than the present value of cash inflows, then the net present value is positive and the rate of return for the project is more than the discount percentage rate (hurdle rate). I is wrong. If the net present value of a project is positive, it would indicate that the rate of return for the project is greater than the discount percentage rate (hurdle rate) used in the net present value computation.

211. (B) Net present value is computed as the difference between project inflows and outflows, discounted to present value as follows:

Inflows Years 1 through 5: $430,000 × 3.83 = $1,646,900
Year 6 inflow: $90,000 × 0.59 = $53,100

Present value of all inflows	$1,700,000
Outflow (today, discount factor of 1.0)	−$1,750,000
Net present value	($50,000)

212. (C) I and II are correct. When the cash flows are the same for both years, use an annuity factor. To calculate the present value of the savings for Years 1 and 2, the factor for the present value of an annuity of $1 for two periods is used. To calculate the present value of the savings for Year 3, the factor for the lump sum of a present value of $1 for three periods is required because an annuity factor cannot be used for Year 3 since the amount of savings is not the same as Years 1 and 2.

213. (B) The internal rate of return method determines the present value factor and related interest rate that yields a net present value equal to zero. The internal rate of return focuses the decision maker on the discount rate at which the present value of the cash inflows equals the initial investment. (A) is wrong. Net present value is computed as the difference between project inflows and outflows, discounted to present value. (C) is wrong. The profitability index is used for capital rationing. The profitability index is the ratio of the present value of the cash inflows to the present value of the net initial investment. Limited capital resources are applied in order of the index until either resources are exhausted or the investment required by the next project exceeds remaining resources.

214. (B) I and II are correct. The internal rate of return method determines the present value factor and related interest rate that yields a net present value equal to zero. In addition, the internal rate of return focuses the decision maker on the discount rate at which the present value of the cash inflows equals the initial investment. III is wrong. Projects with an internal rate of return greater than the hurdle rate should be accepted, as they add value to the firm.

215. (A) I is correct. One of the major strengths of the payback method is that it is easy to understand. The payback method takes the total investment in a project and divides it by its annual cash flows to determine the number of years it will take to gain a return of the initial investment. II is wrong. The payback method does *not* consider the time value of money and, while that is a characteristic of the payback method, it is viewed as a limitation of the payback method and *not* an advantage.

216. (A) I is correct. When using the net present value method of capital budgeting, different hurdle rates can be used for each year of the project. II is wrong. Both the net present value method and the internal rate of return model are discounted cash flow methods.

217. (D) I and II are wrong. The tax depreciation allowance will provide a tax savings, sometimes called a tax shield, that impacts cash flow and must be considered in the net present value analysis. Added working capital requirements will affect cash flow. If supplies need to be purchased to support a new machine, this would reduce cash flow.

218. (A) I, II, and III are correct. The discounted cash flow model is the best for long-term decisions. Discounted cash flow methods include the net present value, internal rate of return, and profitability index. The profitability index is most useful when funds are limited and projects must be selected based on highest returns.

219. (D) I and II are wrong. The accounting rate of return is based on accrual basis income rather than cash flows. It does not consider the time value of money and is considered inferior to the discounted cash flow methods. The payback method takes the total investment in a project and divides it by its annual cash flows to determine the number of years it will

Answers ‹ 169

take to gain a return of the initial investment. The payback method does not consider the time value of money or the return after the initial investment is recovered.

220. (B) Profitability index is measured as:

Present value of net future cash inflows ÷ Present value of net initial investment

Companies hope that this ratio will be higher than 1.0, which means that the present value of the inflows is greater than the present value of the outflows. The profitability index is useful when funds are limited and capital rationing needs to be considered.

221. (B) With even cash flows, payback period is calculated as initial cost divided by annual net cash inflows, or $600,000 ÷ $220,000 = 2.73$.

222. (D) I and II are correct. The payback period computation ignores cash flows after the initial investment has been recovered. The payback method focuses on liquidity and the time it takes to recover the initial investment. The discounted payback period considers the time value of money, but, like any other payback method, it ignores cash flows after the initial investment has been recovered. III is wrong. The net present value method measures the amount of absolute return and, as a result, focuses on cash flows both before and after payback.

223. (A) I is correct. The common disadvantage of all capital budgeting models is their reliance on an uncertain future. Capital financing relates to longer periods of time that are subject to greater levels of uncertainty than other, short-term budgeting decisions. II is wrong. The net present value method and internal rate of return do consider the time value of money, and because this is a characteristic of the net present value method and internal rate of return, this is considered an advantage of those methods rather than a limitation.

224. (D) The discounted payback period is computed as follows:

Year	Net Cash Flows	Factor	PV	Cumulative Payback
1	$9,000	0.943	$8,487	$8,487
2	$15,000	0.841	$12,615	$21,102
3	$19,000	0.776	$14,744	$35,846
4	$25,000	0.719	$17,975	$53,821

Note that the cumulative payback after Year 3 is $35,846. The portion of the fourth year needed to fully pay back the $46,000 cost is computed as the ratio of the amount remaining to be recovered to the amount collected in the fourth year as follows:

$46,000 − $35,846 = $10,154
$10,154 ÷ $17,975 = 0.564

The discounted payback period is:

Years 1–3	3 years
Year 4	+ 0.564 year
Total	3.564 years

225. (B) The internal rate of return is often calculated using trial and error by dividing the investment by the cash inflows to equal a desired present value factor. The internal rate of return is the present value factor that will equate cash inflows to cash outflows. (A) is wrong. The net present value is calculated by subtracting cash outflows from cash inflows; the net present value would only be zero if the cash inflows equal the cash outflows. (C) is wrong. The payback method is not a discounted cash flow method. This method focuses on liquidity and the time it takes to recover the initial investment. (D) is wrong. Accounting rate of return is not a discounted cash flow method. Based on accrual income rather than cash flows, it does not consider the time value of money and is considered inferior to the discounted cash flow methods.

226. (D) I and II are correct. The net present value method assumes that positive cash flows are reinvested at the hurdle rate, thereby considering compounding. The net present value method also measures the value of capital investments in dollars and considers the time value of money. III is wrong. Net present value uses the cash basis, not the accrual basis.

227. (A) I is correct. The payback (and discounted payback) method neglects total project profitability. Payback methods simply look at the time required to recover the initial investment; subsequent cash flows are ignored. II is wrong. The net present value method is useful in calculating the total project profitability. Simply subtract the cash outflows (often just the initial investment) from the present value of the cash inflows.

228. (D) I and III are correct. Taking the total investment and dividing by annual cash flows is useful to determine the payback period. The profitability index can be calculated by dividing the present value of total net future cash inflows by the present value of net cash outflows.

229. (B) The calculation is as follows:

Salvage value expected cash inflow ($15,000 × 0.618)	$9,270
Operating expected cash inflows ($20,000 × 3.847)	+ $76,940
Present value total cash inflows	$86,210

The present value of the cash inflows is $86,210. Cash flows received annually and evenly are discounted using the present value of an annuity, while single cash inflows are discounted using the present value of $1.

230. (D) Net present value is computed as the difference between the present value of the initial cash outflows of the investment and the present value of the cash inflows from the project. Cash flows received annually and evenly are discounted using the present value of an annuity, while single cash inflows are discounted using the present value of $1. Net present value is calculated as follows:

Salvage value ($15,000 × 0.618)	$9,270
Annual cash inflows ($20,000 × 3.847)	+ $76,940
Present value total cash inflows	$86,210
Present value cash outflow	− $90,000
Total net present value	($3,790)

This investment would *not* add value to the firm and should be rejected. Note that present value figures ignore net income and instead focus on cash flow information.

231. (A) The net present value is $27,250 with no salvage value. The only cash flows that are relevant are:

$125,000 × 4.698 present value of five-year annuity discounted at 7% = $587,250
$587,250 − $560,000 investment = $27,250 net present value

The net present value is positive, so the asset should be acquired, as it is expected to add value to the firm.

232. (A) The net present value of an investment is equal to the discounted after-tax cash flows from the investment minus the initial cost of the investment. In this question, the discounted cash flows are $237,992 and the investment was $244,500, yielding a negative (unsatisfactory) net present value of $6,508.

233. (A) The internal rate of return is the rate that provides a zero net present value. The internal rate of return is equal to the discount rate at which the net present value of the investment is equal to zero. The $218,340 present value of after-tax cash flows associated with the investment discounted at 9.5 percent is equal to the cost of the investment, also given at $218,340. The internal rate of return, therefore, is 9.5 percent because at a rate of 9.5 percent, the investment neither makes money nor loses money on a cash flow basis. Note that often the internal rate of return needs to be calculated by trial and error, but in this question, as often happens on the exam, enough information to find the answer is given, although several distracting pieces of useless information were also included.

234. (D) I is correct. Advance determination of management's required return is integral to the development and evaluation of net present value. Project cash flows are discounted based upon a predetermined rate and compared to the investment in the project. The difference is expressed as a positive or negative amount. II is wrong. Internal rate of return is evaluated in relation to management's required hurdle rate after the computation of net present value is done. III is wrong. The accounting rate of return computes a percentage return based upon accrual basis data and does not require a predetermined discount rate.

235. (A) Operating leverage is defined as the degree to which a firm uses fixed operating costs as opposed to variable operating costs. A firm that has high operating leverage has high fixed operating costs and relatively low variable operating costs. A firm with high operating leverage (high fixed costs) must produce enough revenue to cover all those fixed costs. Once a firm with high operating leverage covers those high fixed costs, additional revenue should go straight to operating income since variable costs are so low. (B) is wrong. Operating leverage is defined as the degree to which a firm uses fixed operating costs as opposed to variable operating costs. (C) is wrong. Combined (total) leverage (not operating leverage) results from the use of both fixed operating costs and fixed financing costs to magnify returns to the firm's owners. (D) is wrong. Financial leverage (not operating leverage) is defined as the degree to which a firm uses debt to finance the firm.

236. (B) A firm's degree of operating leverage is calculated by dividing the percentage change in earnings before interest and taxes (EBIT) by percentage change in sales. Operating leverage is defined as the degree to which a firm uses fixed operating costs as opposed to variable operating costs. A firm that has high operating leverage has high fixed operating costs and relatively low variable operating costs and uses this cost structure to amplify the financial results of each additional dollar in sales. For example: If a firm experiences a 33 percent increase in EBIT as a result of an 11 percent increase in sales, the firm's operating leverage is 3. When a firm has high operating leverage, a small increase in revenue can lead to a large increase in profit since fixed costs remain the same.

237. (C) A firm's degree of financial leverage is calculated by taking the percent change in earnings per share divided by the percent change in earnings before interest and taxes. Financial leverage is defined as the degree to which a firm uses debt to finance the firm. (B) is wrong. A firm's degree of operating leverage, not financial leverage, is calculated by dividing the percentage change in EBIT by the percentage change in sales.

238. (A) I is correct. When a firm has a relatively high degree of operating leverage, a small increase in sales can lead to a large increase in profit because fixed costs remain the same over a relevant range. II is wrong. When a firm has a relatively high degree of operating leverage, variable operating costs are low, not high, relative to fixed operating costs; therefore, a small increase in sales could lead to a large increase in profit because fixed costs would be covered already.

239. (A) I is correct. Financial leverage is defined as the degree to which a firm uses debt to finance the firm. II is wrong. Operating leverage is defined as the degree to which a firm relies on fixed operating costs as opposed to variable operating costs.

240. (D) The formula for calculating operating leverage is:

Percent change in earnings before interest and taxes divided by the percent change in sales

From the information given:

$24 \div x =$ degree of operating leverage of 4
$x = 6\%$ increase in sales revenue

241. (C) I and II are correct. Company A has a higher degree of operating leverage than company B. Company A has lower variable operating costs and higher fixed operating costs compared to company B. Calculation of degree of operating leverage for company A = 3:

Increase in EBIT 18 divided by increase in sales 6
Degree of operating leverage for company B = 2
Calculated as:
Increase in EBIT 10 divided by increase in sales 5

242. (C) I and II are correct. A high degree of operating leverage implies that a relatively small change in sales, an increase or decrease, will have a greater effect on profits and shareholder value. The higher the firm's degree of operating leverage, the greater its potential profitability but also the greater risk because it must cover a high fixed cost just to break even. But once it breaks even, sales mean profits!

243. (B) Multiplying the operating leverage times the financial leverage equals the combined leverage. Another way of calculating combined leverage is to divide percent change in earnings per share by percent change in sales. (A) is wrong. Multiply (don't add) the operating leverage times the financial leverage to get total combined leverage. (C) is wrong. Dividing the percent change in earnings before interest and taxes by percent change in sales will result in the operating leverage. (D) is wrong. Dividing the percent change in earnings per share by the percent change in EBIT is the financial leverage.

244. (B) I is correct. Financial leverage is defined as the degree to which a firm uses debt to finance the firm. II is wrong. Operating leverage is defined as the degree to which a firm uses fixed operating costs as opposed to variable operating costs. III is wrong. Combined (total) leverage results from the use of both fixed operating costs and fixed financing costs to magnify returns to the firm's owners.

245. (D) The cost of debt capital is computed on an after-tax basis because interest expense is tax deductible. The cost of debt is computed on an after-tax basis using the effective interest rate instead of the coupon rate:

Effective interest rate $13\% \times 0.6^* = 7.8\%$

246. (B) The calculation is as follows:

Weighted average cost of debt capital = 30% weight × 10% interest cost
$0.1 \times (1 - 0.25) = 7.5\% \times 30\%$ weight = 2.25% cost of debt capital

The optimal cost of capital is the ratio of debt to equity that produces the lowest weighted average cost of capital (WACC). Required rates of return by debt and equity holders fluctuate as the ratio of debt to equity changes.

247. (D) Weighted average cost of 10% preferred stock × 10% weight = 1%.

248. (A) Weighted average cost of common stock is equal to its 60% weight × 0.1 = 6%.

249. (C) The weighted average cost of capital is 9.25 percent, calculated as follows:

Weighted average cost of debt capital = 30% weight × 10% interest cost
$0.1 \times (1 - 0.25) = 7.5\% \times 30\%$ weight = 2.25% cost of debt capital
Weighted average cost of 10% preferred stock × 10% weight = 1%
Weighted average cost of common stock is equal to its 60% weight × 0.1 = 6%
Total weighted average cost of capital = 9.25%

To maximize shareholder wealth, the company will most likely establish a hurdle rate that will limit acceptance of projects to only those with minimum returns greater than the WACC of 9.25 percent.

250. (C) I and II are correct. The weighted average cost of capital is the average cost of debt plus the average cost of equity financing given the firm's existing assets and operations. The weighted average cost of capital is determined by weighing each specific type of capital by its proportion to the firm's total capital structure.

---

*1 − 0.4 tax rate = 0.6

251. (C) I and II are correct. The optimal cost of capital is the ratio of debt to equity that produces the lowest weighted average cost of capital. Required rates of return by debt and equity holders fluctuate as the ratio of debt to equity changes. At some point as total debt increases in relation to equity, investors will demand a greater return because the risk of default on the debt increases. With that risk, the creditors will demand a premium in the form of higher returns.

252. (C) The risk-free rate is 5 percent, and the market return is 12 percent. If you invested in the stock market, you would demand a premium of 7 percent beyond the risk-free rate, but the 7 percent market premium is only correct if the stock had a beta equal to the overall market, 1.0. Since the beta for this stock is less than 1.0, multiply the beta for the stock, which is 0.95, by the market risk premium of 7 percent, and 6.65 percent is the market risk premium for this stock. Then add the risk-free rate of 5 percent; the appropriate rate of return for this stock is 11.65 percent.

$$5\% + 0.95\,(12\% - 5\%)$$
$$= 5\% + (0.95 \times 7\%)$$
$$= 5\% + 6.65\% = 11.65\%$$

253. (B) II is correct. Interest expense is a tax deduction; therefore, the cost to Valley Corporation is lower than the market yield rate on debt. I is wrong. If market interest rates increase, then Valley's bonds would have to be offered at a discount to stay competitive with the market. This discount would increase (not lower) Valley's cost of debt.

254. (A) The risk-free rate is 7 percent and the market return is estimated at 12.4 percent. If you invested in the stock market, you would demand a premium of 5.4 percent, but a 5.4 percent premium is not good enough for this stock because the beta for this stock is 1.2. Multiply the 5.4 percent market risk premium by the 1.2 beta; the appropriate risk premium for this stock is 6.48 percent. Take the 6.48 percent and add the risk-free rate of 7 percent; the appropriate rate of return for this stock is 13.48 percent.

Cost of retained earnings $= 0.07 + 1.2\,(0.124 - 0.07)$
$1.2 \times 0.054 = 0.0648$
$0.07 + 0.0648 = 13.48\%$

255. (C) I and II are correct. The capital asset pricing model is used to calculate cost of retained earnings (cost of common equity). The discounted cash flow model also is used to calculate the cost of common equity. The forecasted dividend is divided by the current market price and then a growth rate is added.

256. (A) 14 percent. Using the discounted cash flow (DCF) method, the cost of equity is computed as follows:

Cost of equity = Expected dividend ÷ Current share price + Growth rate
($4 ÷ $50) + 0.06 = 0.08 + 0.06 = 0.14

Note that the cost of equity is not computed on an after-tax basis. Dividends are not tax deductible. Also, if the dividend given was the "current dividend" rather than the "next dividend," then to determine the numerator, the current dividend would need to be multiplied by the dividend growth rate of 6 percent because the numerator is the forecasted dividend rather than the current dividend.

257. (B) The current ratio is found by dividing current assets by current liabilities. The result is a measure of a firm's ability to pay short-term obligations as they become due. When a firm cannot meet current obligations as they become due, the firm can be forced into bankruptcy by its creditors. For this reason, the current ratio is seen as a critical measure of a firm's liquidity.

258. (B) II is correct. Declaring a stock dividend would only impact the stockholders' equity section of the balance sheet. I is wrong. The current ratio is current assets divided by current liabilities. The sale of equipment would increase cash and, therefore, increase current assets without increasing current liabilities. As a result, the sale of equipment would increase the current ratio.

259. (C) Net working capital is the difference between current assets and current liabilities. Current assets went up $100,000, so working capital increases. Current liabilities went down by $35,000, also increasing working capital. The net effect is an increase in net working capital of $135,000.

260. (D) Return on investment (ROI) is the ratio of operating income to average operating assets. The denominator is beginning operating assets plus ending operating assets divided by 2. Although simple to calculate, ROI is not the best measure of investment performance because ROI sometimes encourages shortsighted behavior that defers or avoids investment with a (low) positive return for the sake of current ROI performance.

261. (B) Return on investment for Year 5 is equal to:

Operating income for Year 5 ($200,000* ÷ $1,100,000**)   18.18%

262. (A) When calculating return on investments (ROI), the higher the denominator, the lower the return. In calculating ROI, the denominator is average assets. Using replacement cost to value average assets will better compare company A to company B because replacement cost ignores age of assets and method of depreciation. (B) is wrong. Per GAAP rules, the net book value can be used, but that would be skewed by age of assets and method of depreciation. A company using accelerated depreciation would have a lower book value and, therefore, higher return. (C) is wrong. Gross book value would ignore the method of depreciation but still would be skewed by age of assets. A company with fully depreciated older assets would have a lower denominator and, therefore, a higher return. (D) is wrong. You should probably use liquidation value if the companies are going bankrupt, but there is no evidence that these companies are going bankrupt.

263. (B) II is correct. Using the residual income method, net income per the income statement is compared to the required rate of return. The result is the dollar amount of residual income. Residual income is the excess of net income over the desired amount of return for the project or investment center. I is wrong. Return on investment (ROI) calculates a percentage return, not a dollar amount of return. Although ROI is simple to calculate, there is a weakness of using it to evaluate the performance of investment center managers. The weakness is that ROI may lead to managers rejecting projects that yield positive cash flows yet have a low ROI percentage. Profitable investment center managers might be reluctant

---

*$900,000 − $700,000 = $200,000
**$1,100,000 is average operating assets, calculated as ($900,000 + $1,300,000) ÷ 2 = $1,100,000

to invest in projects that might lower their ROI (especially if their bonuses are based only on their investment center's ROI), even though those projects might generate positive cash flows for the company as a whole. This characteristic is often known as the "disincentive to invest." Therefore, a different method of rating an investment center manager's performance, known as the residual income method, is often used instead of ROI.

264. (B) Residual income is the difference between net income and the required return. The required return is net book value (total assets) times the hurdle rate (required rate of return). The calculations are as follows:

Division	Operating Income	Total Assets × Required Rate	Residual Net Income
J	$150	$1,000 × 0.09 = $90	$60
K	$300	$1,200 × 0.09 = $108	$192
Totals	$450	$198	$252

265. (A) The calculation is as follows:

Divisional revenues	$1,000,000
Divisional expenses	− $600,000
Divisional income	$400,000
Division assets	$2,000,000
Required return	× 15%
Hurdle	($300,000)
Residual income	$100,000
Bonus rate	× 25%
Bonus amount	$25,000

266. (A) I is correct. Economic value added (EVA) is essentially similar to the residual income method, as both measure investment performance in terms of dollars rather than percentages using net income minus the desired return. The difference between the two is what is being used as the hurdle rate to determine desired return. II is wrong. Using EVA, the hurdle rate must be the weighted average cost of capital. Note that EVA makes for a more objective measure of investment performance than residual income because using the residual income method, the hurdle rate can be set by management or management can use the weighted average cost of capital as the hurdle rate. Using residual income, judgment may need to be used if the hurdle rate set by management is too high or too low. The weakness of residual income compared to EVA is that if management sets the hurdle rate, management needs to use judgment to set a hurdle rate that is achievable to motivate the investment manager. Using EVA, this is not a problem because EVA relies on weighted average cost of capital (WACC) as the hurdle rate, and weighted average cost of capital is more objective for determining the hurdle rate than simply allowing management to set the hurdle rate.

267. (B) II is correct. Residual income is an accrual method, a dollar amount of net income in excess of a desired amount. Other accrual basis methods of investment measurement include return on investment and economic value added. I is wrong. Net present value is based on cash flows, not accrual accounting.

268. (C) I and II are correct. The weighted average cost of capital is frequently used as the hurdle rate within capital budgeting techniques. Investments that provide a return that exceeds the weighted average cost of capital should continuously add value to the firm. Weighted average cost of capital is most commonly compared to the internal rate of return to evaluate whether to make an investment. The internal rate of return is the rate of return that sets cash outflows to cash inflows.

269. (C) I and II are correct. Increased economic uncertainty would cause a firm to decrease debt (and interest cost), so decreased economic uncertainty would provide the incentive for firms to borrow more. An increase in the corporate income tax rate might cause a firm to increase the debt in its financial structure because interest is tax deductible, while dividends are not.

270. (A) I is correct. The optimal capital structure is the mix of financing instruments that produces the lowest weighted average cost of capital. A company with a low weighted average cost of capital is attractive to potential shareholders. II is wrong. The company's borrowing rate is a component of the weighted average cost of capital, along with the cost of common stock, preferred stock, and retained earnings. At some point as the debt to equity ratio increases, investors will demand a greater return as leverage becomes more pronounced and debtors will require compensation for the high level of default risk.

271. (D) I and II are wrong. Not a decrease but rather an increase in the cost of carrying inventory would lead to a reduction in average inventory. For example, dairy products are required to be refrigerated so that they will not spoil. If electricity prices are rising, management would prefer to have a lower inventory of fresh dairy products on hand because of the electricity (i.e., carrying) cost of the items. Increased demand would likely increase average inventory to avoid the cost of running out of desired items, known as stockout costs.

272. (D) I and II are wrong. Inventory turnover is an activity ratio used to evaluate the efficiency of the firm, not profitability. Inventory turnover is calculated by taking the number of days in the year, 365, divided by inventory turnover to equal "days of inventory on hand." Debt to total assets measures solvency, not profitability.

273. (C) I and II are correct. A quick ratio is a measure of a firm's liquidity. Quick ratio is current assets minus inventory divided by current liabilities. Quick ratio recognizes the fact that inventory cannot be used to pay bills. Quick ratio is a better measure of liquidity than current ratio because it shows how a firm can satisfy current obligations without packaging up inventory and sending it to creditors to settle debts. A company's average collection period is used to evaluate the liquidity of the firm through the calculation of the cash conversion cycle.

274. (C) The calculation for weighted average cost of capital is:

Preferred equity 20% weight, 9% yield	1.8%
Common equity 40% weight, 12% yield	+ 4.8%
Debt 40% × 6% × (1 − 0.3)	+ 1.7%
Weighted average cost of capital	8.3%

275. (A) I is correct. A company's debt to total capital ratio includes in the denominator interest-bearing debt plus equity. II is wrong. Noninterest-bearing debt is not included in the denominator of the debt to total capital ratio. Debt to total capital ratio equals debt divided by interest-bearing debt plus equity.

276. (A) I is correct. The quick ratio is current assets minus inventory divided by current liabilities. Purchasing inventory through the issuance of long-term notes would have no impact on the quick ratio. Inventory is excluded from the numerator of the quick ratio, and long-term debt is excluded from the denominator of the quick ratio. II is wrong. Selling inventory would increase the quick ratio. The addition of cash would increase the numerator with no impact on current liabilities.

277. (C) The calculation is as follows:

$180,000 × 0.11 = $19,800 interest paid
$19,800 interest paid ÷ $180,000 loan × 0.8 net of 20% compensating balance = $144,000 net proceeds.
Therefore $19,800 ÷ $144,000 = 13.75%.

When a bank requires a 20% compensating balance, the net proceeds are only 80% of the loan.

278. (D) II is correct. The growth rate of earnings is *not* part of the calculation of cost of equity. Three elements are needed to calculate the cost of equity capital: current dividends, market price of stock, and growth rate in dividends (not growth rate in earnings). A firm's cost of equity represents the compensation that the market demands in exchange for bearing the risk of ownership.

279. (D) The calculation for cost of equity capital is:

$2 expected dividend next period ÷ $20 stock price	10%
Growth rate	+ 11.5%
Cost of equity capital	21.5%

280. (B) The current ratio is current assets divided by current liabilities. The sale of property, plant, and equipment would increase cash and, therefore, current assets without increasing current liabilities. This would increase the current ratio. Furthermore, the sale of equipment at a loss would decrease net income.

281. (B) Average inventory is computed as the sum of beginning and ending inventory divided by 2, as follows:

($350,500 + $259,100) ÷ 2 = $304,800

Inventory turnover is the ratio of cost of goods sold to average inventory, computed as follows:

Cost of Goods Sold	Average Inventory	Inventory Turnover
$1,500,000	÷ $304,800	= 4.92

282. (C) Cost savings would be calculated by dividing cost of goods sold by actual inventory turnover and then by desired inventory turnover, as follows:

$3,800,000 ÷ 7 =	$542,857
$3,800,000 ÷ 9	− $422,222
Inventory decrease	$120,635
Interest rate	× 6%
Cost savings	$7,238

283. (A) Annual percentage cost of not taking the discount is equal to 360 divided by the (total pay period minus the discount period) times discount divided by (100% minus discount).

$360/(30 − 10) × 4\%/(100\% − 4\%)$
$= 360/20 × 4\%/(96\%)$
$= 18 × 4.17\% = 75.06\%$

Note that the formula to determine the cost of not paying within the discount period appears above. The formula would be the same if calculating the cost of offering a discount to customers in exchange for their quick payment.

284. (D) Annual cost of not taking the discount is equal to 360 divided by the (total pay period minus the discount period) times discount divided by (100% minus discount).

$360/(30 − 10) × 3\%/(100\% − 3\%)$
$= 360/20 × 3.09\%$
$= 18 × 3.09\% = 55.62\%$

The formula to determine the cost of not paying within the discount period would be the same if calculating the cost of offering a discount.

285. (B) A lockbox system generally relates to expediting deposits over a specific group of transactions. The technique arranges for the direct mailing of customers' remittances to a bank's post office box and subsequent deposit. (A) is wrong. Concentration banking is the method by which a single bank is designated as a central bank. Concentration banking improves controls. Having all bank accounts in a single bank makes it easier to keep track of inflows and outflows. (C) is wrong. Zero balance banking doesn't control cash receipts; instead it represents an account that maintains a zero balance like a payroll account that receives money from a master account in time for employees to be paid and otherwise contains a zero balance. Zero balance banking serves to maximize the availability of idle cash, not control receipts. (D) is wrong. Compensating balances do not establish better control over cash receipts. Compensating balances are minimum balances maintained by a customer of a bank to avoid bank charges or eliminate fees for credit lines.

286. (D) Using the lockbox produces a savings of $10,000 per year, as calculated below:

Lockbox cost	− $50,000
Investment income	+ $60,000*
Savings per year	$10,000

With a lockbox system, customers of the firm mail checks directly to the bank. Banks will charge a fee. The benefit is that the money immediately begins earning interest. A lockbox is a way to get paid sooner, but only use a lockbox if the interest income exceeds the bank fees.

---

*$60,000 = (3 days ÷ 360 days) × $80,000,000 × 0.09

287. (B) The calculation is as follows:

Average daily cash outflows	$1,000,000
Days added to disbursement schedule	× 3
Excess funds	$3,000,000
Interest rate on excess funds	× 6%
Maximum allowable cost	$180,000

288. (B) A company's cash conversion cycle is the average number of days to create cash from core operations. The formula for cash conversion cycle is number of days to sell inventory (low number!) plus number of days to collect (hopefully another low number!) minus the number of days to pay vendor (high number!). The cash conversion cycle is the sum of the inventory conversion and receivable collection periods minus the payables deferral period. A lower cash conversion cycle is better than a higher cycle.

289. (A) I and II are correct. Decreasing inventory conversion and accounts receivable collection periods indicate that cash is being collected more quickly than last year from sales of inventory and from faster collections of accounts receivable. III is wrong. An increasing deferral period on payables indicates that the cash disbursements are being deferred (held as long as possible).

290. (A) A higher inventory turnover from one year to the next means a lower inventory conversion. That is a positive since it takes fewer days in Year 2 to move inventory compared to Year 1. In the following example, all numbers are in millions:

Year 1	Cost of goods sold 27 ÷ 5 average inventory
Inventory turnover	5.4×
Year 1 conversion	365 days ÷ 5.4× = 67.6 days to sell inventory in Year 1

Year 2—For turnover to be higher in Year 2, let's say average inventory falls to $4 million from $5 million.

Cost of goods sold	$27
Average inventory	$4

Result would be a higher annual turnover of 6.75× (good news) and a lower inventory conversion period, 365 ÷ 6.75 = 54.07. This means that it took only 54 days to sell inventory in Year 2 compared to 67 days in Year 1; that's a positive. The goal is to minimize inventory but not too low. Inventory needs to be high enough to meet demand but no higher, because excess inventory adds no value to a firm; it only adds costs.

291. (B) II is correct. The amount of inventory a company would tend to hold in stock would decrease as the length of time that goods are in transit decreases. If goods ordered could arrive the next day, for example, inventory levels could be minimized and resupplied quickly. I is wrong. The amount of inventory a company would tend to hold in stock would decrease as the cost of running out of stock decreases. If stockout costs were high, inventory would be higher, not lower.

292. (D) The 50,000 cards sold per year divided by 50 weeks equals an average of 1,000 cards being sold per week. Then, 1,000 cards sold per week times four weeks lead time equals 4,000 cards sold during the time it takes to place and receive an order from Hallmark. If the safety stock is 750 cards, the reorder point is 4,750.

293. (B) I and II are correct. In a just in time system, products are produced just in time to be sold. Therefore, just in time systems maintain a much smaller level of inventory when compared to traditional systems. Inventory turnover (cost of goods sold divided by average inventory) increases with a switch to just in time. III is wrong. Inventory as a percentage of total assets decreases rather than increases with a switch from a traditional to a just in time inventory system.

294. (C) I and II are correct. High carrying costs would decrease safety stock. Lower stock-out costs would decrease safety stock.

295. (D) I, II, and III are correct. The optimal level of inventory is affected by the time required to receive inventory. If lead times become more variable, the amount of safety stock needed to reduce the risk of stockouts will increase. The optimal level of inventory is affected by the cost per unit of inventory, which will have a direct impact on inventory carrying costs. The cost of placing an order impacts order frequency, which affects order size and, therefore, affects optimal inventory levels. IV is wrong. The current amount of inventory has no impact on the optimal level.

296. (C) I and II are correct. The economic order quantity (EOQ) method of inventory control anticipates orders at the point where carrying costs are nearest to restocking costs. The objective of EOQ is to minimize total inventory costs.

297. (D) I and II are wrong. A reduction in accounts receivable would serve to improve (increase) the turnover ratio. Factoring (selling) receivables would serve to reduce the amount of accounts receivable (indicating more rapid collections). Factoring receivables would increase (improve) the company's accounts receivable turnover ratio. The accounts receivable turnover ratio is expressed as sales divided by accounts receivable.

298. (A) Accounts receivable turnover is calculated as sales divided by average receivables.

$$\$105,000 \div \$14,000 = 7.5$$

Average receivables is calculated as beginning accounts receivable plus ending accounts receivable divided by 2.

$$\$15,000 + \$13,000 = \$28,000$$
$$\$28,000 \div 2 = \$14,000$$

299. (C) I and II are correct. With the economic order quantity (EOQ), the carrying cost per unit is anticipated to remain constant and the cost of placing an order is anticipated to remain constant. The EOQ is a formula that allows managers to calculate the ideal quantity of inventory to order for a given product. The calculation is designed to minimize ordering and carrying costs.

300. (A) I is correct. The question asked which of the following would *not* be relevant to economic order quantity (EOQ). The purchase price per unit is not a component of EOQ but rather the cost per purchase order. II is wrong. Annual sales volume *is* a key variable in the EOQ formula. The components of the EOQ formula include demand in units for the product, the ordering cost per purchase order, and the carrying cost for one unit.

301. (B) II is correct. In the economic order quantity, carrying costs are calculated per unit. I is wrong. In the economic order quantity, ordering costs are calculated per order, not per unit.

302. (B) The calculation is as follows:

Economic order quantity = $\sqrt{(2 \times \text{annual demand} \times \text{ordering costs}) \div \text{carrying costs}}$
= $\sqrt{(2 \times 2{,}400 \times (\$50)) \div 3}$
Economic order quantity = $\sqrt{(\$240{,}000 \div 3)} = \$80{,}000$
Economic order quantity = $\sqrt{\$80{,}000}$
Economic order quantity = 282.84 (rounded to 283)

Notice that the $35 price per pair is not used in the economic order quantity (EOQ) calculation since EOQ is based on cost per order, not cost per unit.

Chapter 4: Information Technology

303. (A) I is correct. An exception report is a report produced when a specific condition or "exception" occurs. II is wrong. An ad hoc report is a report that does not currently exist but that needs to be created on demand without having to get a software developer involved.

304. (C) I and II are correct. Grandfather, father, and son files can be used to recover from processing problems by reverting back to files prior to when they became corrupt. Grandfather, father, and son files can be used to retain files off-site for disaster recovery. As the most recent file is stored, the oldest is killed off.

305. (D) There is no greater level of control necessary for batch processing versus online real-time (online) processing. Online processing (online, real-time [OLRT] processing) is an immediate processing method in which each transaction goes through all processing steps (data entry, data validation, and master file update) before the next transaction is processed. These OLRT files are always current, and error detection is immediate. (A) and (C) are wrong. For batch processing, stored data would only be current if no changes to the data have been made since the last batch update. (B) is wrong. Online real-time transactions are processed in real time, *not* on a periodic basis.

306. (C) I and II are correct. An AIS is best suited to solve problems where there is certainty along with clearly defined reporting requirements. The first step in an AIS is that transaction data from source documents are entered into the AIS by an end user. While AIS systems generally have similar capabilities, the applications implemented for a particular business are generally modified to meet the specific needs of that business. For example, the requirements of a retail warehouse club would be different from those of a CPA firm.

307. (C) The final step is the financial reports are generated. The steps in an AIS are:

The transaction data from source documents are entered into the AIS by an end user.
The original paper source documents are filed.
These transactions are recorded in the appropriate journal.
The transactions are posted to the general and subsidiary ledgers.
Trial balances are prepared.
Financial reports are generated.

308. (D) I is correct. A characteristic of a centralized processing system is that processing is consistent because it is all handled at the central location. II is wrong. In a centralized processing system, there is a need for increased, not decreased, processing power and data storage at the central location. III is wrong. In a centralized processing system, there can be a reduction in local accountability.

309. (D) I and II are wrong. While a decrease in local accountability is a characteristic of centralized processing, this is *not* an advantage but a disadvantage of centralized processing. Increased power and storage needs at the centralized location are other disadvantages of centralized processing.

310. (B) II is correct. Business information systems allow a business to collect data, process data, store and transform data, and distribute data. Hardware, software, network, people, and data are components of a business information system. I is wrong. Data initiation is not part of a business information system.

311. (C) I, III, IV, and V are correct. The business information system includes software, hardware, data, and people. Reports are *not* one of the components of a business information system. Network, also a part of a business information system, was not listed in the question.

312. (C) IV and V are correct. Data initiation and data reporting are not part of a business information system. Business information systems allow a business to perform the following functions on data: collect, process, store, transform, and distribute.

313. (A) I is correct. The question asked which of the following is *not* correct. Production and test data are stored in different databases. II is wrong. Access to production data is less open than access to test data. Since this is a true statement, II is an incorrect choice.

314. (B) Block coding represents assignment of blocks of numbers to broad categories of items (e.g., a general ledger chart of accounts that assigns stockholders' equity to the 2000 series of account numbers, revenue to the 3000 series of account numbers, expenses to the 4000 series, and so on). (A) is wrong, as sequential coding simply numbers documents, transactions, or other items in order (sequence). A stack of preprinted checks is an example of sequential coding; the first check is #101, the next is #102, and so on. (C) is wrong. Group coding embeds intelligence into the identification numbers associated with a particular item. A driver's license number, for example, contains intelligence about the driver's name and eye color and whether the driver wears glasses.

315. (C) Fields represent the first phase of computer storage. Fields (e.g., numerals and letters) comprise records (e.g., names and addresses) that are organized into files (such as the approved vendor list) that create databases (e.g., for an accounts payable listing).

316. (A) I is correct. Data storage is a major function of transaction processing along with data input, data processing, and information output. II is wrong. Analysis of data is not a major function of transaction processing. Analysis is typically performed after transaction processing.

317. **(C)** I and II are correct. The SEC's Interactive Data Rule requires public companies to present financial statements and related exhibits using XBRL, which is specifically designed to exchange financial information over the web.

318. **(D)** I and II are wrong. Program modification controls include controls that attempt to prevent changes by unauthorized personnel. In addition, program modification controls track program changes so that there is an exact record of what versions of what programs were running in production at any specific point in time.

319. **(B)** II is correct. The duties of systems programmers and application programmers should be segregated. The duties of systems analysts and application programmers are often combined, which is fine.

320. **(C)** Support is keeping the system up and running. Support includes monitoring the system, determining that a problem has occurred, and fixing or getting around the problem. (A) is wrong. Maintenance refers to keeping the system "up to date" with new releases from time to time. (B) is wrong. Support (not maintenance) includes monitoring the system, determining that a problem has occurred, and fixing or getting around the problem. (D) is wrong. Maintenance refers to keeping the system "up to date" with new releases from time to time.

321. **(D)** I is correct. In a structured system, each program within a system is independent of other programs within the system. This enables programming teams to work independently on different programs within the same system. II is wrong. Management reporting systems provide managers with the information needed for day-to-day decision-making. III is wrong. Interactive systems are computer-based information systems that provide interactive support to managers or others during the decision-making process.

322. **(D)** A hardware technician sets up and configures computers. (A) is wrong. Users are any workers who enter data into a system or who use the information processed by the system. Users could be employees as well as outside consultants such as accountants, auditors, etc. (B) is wrong. A software developer designs the systems and writes the programs to collect, process, store, transform, and distribute the data and information entered by the users. (C) is wrong. A network administrator sets up and configures a computer network so that multiple computers can share the same data and information.

323. **(B)** Sensitivity analysis is a decision support system that uses a "what-if" technique that asks how a given outcome will change if the original estimates of the model are changed. (A) is wrong. Scenario analysis allows an analyst or manager to look at possible outcomes and predict a value given the probability of each outcome occurring. (C) is wrong. Database query applications read and reorganize data to management's specifications but do not allow alterations of the data. (D) is wrong. A financial modeling application is used to assist management in evaluating financing alternatives.

324. **(B)** II and III are correct. A Trojan horse poses a security risk. A Trojan horse is software that appears to have a useful function but contains a hidden and unintended function that presents a security risk when the computer program is run. A backdoor represents a security risk because a backdoor is a means of access to a program or system that bypasses normal security measures and therefore should be eliminated. I is wrong, as a web crawler poses no security risk. A web crawler is a program that browses the Internet to create copies of visited web pages for later processing by a search engine.

325. (B) I and III are correct. Network maintenance and wireless access are both responsibilities of the network administrator. II is wrong. A database administrator designs the firm's database and controls it. His or her duties generally include maintaining security measures.

326. (A) An application programmer is the person responsible for writing and/or maintaining application programs and should not be responsible for controlling or handling data.

327. (D) A systems analyst designs the overall application system. The systems analyst is authorized to design the system, and that role should be segregated from the custody of the program, which will belong to the librarian. (A) is wrong. The librarian has a custodian role over the program, not an authorization role. (B) is wrong. A computer operator has a record-keeping job rather than authorization. (C) is wrong. Programmers have a record-keeping function rather than an authorization function.

328. (B) II is correct. A system programmer is responsible for installing, supporting, monitoring, and maintaining the operating system. I is wrong. An application programmer is responsible for writing or maintaining application programs.

329. (B) II is correct. The reliability business requirement for information includes the criterion that information be appropriate to operate the entity. I is wrong. The business requirement known as availability includes the criteria that information be available currently and in the future and that resources be safeguarded. The control objectives for information and related technology (COBIT) framework identifies seven information criteria: integrity, confidentiality, efficiency, reliability, availability, compliance, and effectiveness.

330. (A) I is correct. The integrity business requirement for information includes the criteria that information be accurate, complete, and valid. II is wrong. Within the context of business requirements for information, efficiency concerns delivery of information through the optimal use of resources (e.g., low cost without compromising effectiveness). The control objectives for information and related technology (COBIT) framework identifies seven information criteria: integrity, confidentiality, efficiency, reliability, availability, compliance, and effectiveness.

331. (D) Along with value delivery, the focus areas identified by the control objectives for information and related technology (COBIT) framework for IT governance include:

Strategic alignment
Resource management
Risk management
Performance measurement

332. (D) I and II are wrong. Hardware, networking, and system software are part of IT infrastructure.

333. (C) The monitor and evaluate domain relates to ensuring that directions are followed and providing feedback to information criteria.

334. (B) II is correct. Using the control objectives for information and related technology (COBIT) framework, the "deliver and support" domain relates to the delivery of the IT service. I is wrong. The "acquire and implement" domain relates to the delivery of the IT solution.

335. (A) I and II are correct. When changing from a manual system to a computer system, internal control objectives and principles do not change. Whether using a manual or computerized system, the objectives and principles are still safeguarding assets and segregating duties. III is wrong. While safeguarding assets and segregating duties remain the same, the implementation of the principles is different. Specific controls will need to change when switching from a manual system of controls to a computerized system.

336. (C) A systems analyst would take on the role of learning a purchased software application and would have the job of integrating it into any existing software. The systems analyst would also take responsibility for training staff.

337. (D) I and II are wrong. Automated systems do not eliminate the need to reconcile control accounts and subsidiary ledgers. If a reconciliation were needed in a manual system, it would still be needed in a computerized system.

338. (D) I and II are wrong. I describes management information systems, not executive support systems. Executive support systems provide senior executives information to assist the executives in strategic issues such as nonroutine decisions that may involve analysis of cyclical data, acquisitions, and competitor behavior. II describes transaction processing rather than executive support systems.

339. (A) Within an IT system, the steering committee is charged with developing long-range plans and directing application development and computer operations. (B) is wrong. A systems analyst is generally responsible for designing systems, preparing specifications for programmers, and serving as an intermediary between users and programmers. (C) is wrong. System programmers would be involved in the selection of system software and would be responsible for maintaining system software, including operating systems, network software, and the data management system. (D) is wrong. End users are typically responsible for maintaining control over the completeness, accuracy, and distribution of input and output, not the systems analyst.

340. (C) The independent verification of payroll transactions that typically occurs using parallel processing of transactions represents one of the most effective methods to reduce the risk of incorrect processing of transactions in a newly installed payroll system. Payroll should be processed by the new system and by another system, possibly the old system, and results should be compared. I is wrong. While segregation of duties ensures that the same person cannot both perpetrate and conceal fraud, it does not minimize the risk of incorrect processing due to implementation of a new system. II is wrong. Authorization of transactions is a strong control over the validity or legitimacy of overtime but does not reduce the risk of incorrect processing due to implementation of a new system.

341. (B) Encryption involves using a password or a digital key to scramble a readable (plain text) message into an unreadable (cipher text) message. Data encryption is based on the concept of keys. The length of the key is extremely important in data encryption. The longer the key, the harder it is to crack.

342. (D) All three choices are forms of data security. Password management is a method of preventing intrusion since it regulates system access. Data encryption also is a method of preventing intrusion since it uses a password or a digital key to scramble any readable data into a message unreadable to the potential hacker. Data encryption is, in fact, based on the concept of keys. However, the length of the key is extremely important in data encryption. The longer the key, the harder it is to crack. The algorithm is important, but the length of the key is more important. Finally, digital certificates are forms of data security. Digital certificates are electronic documents created and digitally signed by a trusted party that certifies the identity of the owners of a particular public key.

343. (A) Transactions sent over a value-added network (VAN) are batched periodically rather than as they occur. (B) is wrong. A VAN is superior to the Internet in terms of disaster recovery because records of electronic data interchange (EDI) transactions may be kept for months or years, which can aid in the disaster recovery process. (C) is wrong. The Internet permits EDI transactions to be sent to trading partners as transactions occur.

344. (A) The objectives of customer relationship management (CRM) systems are to increase customer satisfaction and, therefore, increase revenue. A CRM enables the entity to analyze the behavior of customers. (B) is wrong. Electronic data interchange (EDI) is the computer-to-computer exchange of business data in structured format that allows direct processing of the data by the receiving system. It is not an internal communication but always between two separate businesses. (C) is wrong. Decision support systems (DSS) are computer-based information systems that provide interactive support to managers or others during the decision-making process. (D) is wrong. Public key infrastructure (PKI) refers to the system and processes used to issue and manage asymmetric keys and digital certificates.

345. (C) I and II are correct. Electronic data interchange (EDI) transactions may be transmitted using a value-added network (VAN) or by the Internet. A VAN would be more costly because privately operated VANs charge user fees.

346. (C) I and II are correct. The cost of sending electronic data interchange (EDI) transactions using a value-added network is greater than the cost of using the Internet. In addition, EDI requires strict adherence to a standard data format. Translation software is required to convert internal company data to the strict standard format. This translation software must either be purchased or be internally developed.

347. (C) II and III are correct. Just because the merchant cannot see the physical credit card, there are still privacy issues. A credit card cannot be used to pay for goods or services online while maintaining (complete) financial privacy. Even a very secure site does not guarantee privacy. An electronic check may allow for faster payment but does not guarantee privacy. Electronic checks contain all the same financial information that paper checks contain, so there is no additional privacy with an electronic check. I is wrong. E-cash is currency in an electronic form that maintains financial privacy just as real cash does.

348. (C) Encryption is the encoding of data for security purposes. (A) is wrong. Decoding is the process used by the recipient of encoded information to decipher the message with use of an electronic "key." (B) is wrong. Mapping is the process of determining the correspondence between elements in a company's format and elements in standard electronic data interchange format. (D) is wrong. Translation is the conversion of data from one format to another. Once the mapping has been completed, translation software can be developed to convert transactions from one format to the other.

349. (C) I and II are correct. The two most important controls in an electronic data interchange (EDI) environment are activity trails of failed transactions and network and sender recipient acknowledgments.

350. (D) Internet transactions are faster, less expensive, and less secure than electronic data interchange (EDI) transactions over a value-added network (VAN). This is because the VAN is more secure and there is a price to pay for those controls.

351. (D) Cloud computing involves having virtual servers available over the Internet for storing hardware and software. This allows a company to expand its IT capabilities. Cost savings are expected over the long term. (A) is wrong. Domain name warehousing is the practice of obtaining control over domain names for possible future use. (B) is wrong. Secure socket layer is what encrypts certain data in conjunction with HTTP; for example, credit card data must be encrypted. (C) is wrong. Hypertext transfer protocol allows for sound, video, and images to be transferred over the Internet.

352. (A) The risk of choosing inappropriate technology is known as strategic risk. (B) is wrong. Operating risk is the risk of doing the right thing but in the wrong sequential order. (C) is wrong. Financial risk includes the risk of having assets wasted, stolen, or lost. (D) is wrong. Information risk includes the risk of lost data, computer crashes, and hackers.

353. (A) I is correct. In a denial-of-service attack, one computer bombards another computer with a flood of information intended to keep legitimate users from accessing the target computer or network. II is wrong. A Trojan horse, not phishing, is a program that appears to have a useful function but that contains a hidden and unintended function that presents a security risk. Phishing represents phony e-mails sent to recipients in order to gain access to the unknowing recipient's banking information.

354. (D) No password is perfect, but of the passwords listed, 2456dtR5! is the most difficult to crack because it contains a combination of small letters, capital letters, numbers, and other characters, known as ascii.

355. (C) I and II are correct. Limit tests set a numeric limit, a ceiling for processing, such as no payroll check allowed more than $5,000. The limit is $5,000, and any payroll check requested in excess of $5,000 should *not* be processed, but rather an exception report should be generated. A validity check is an input control that would prevent or detect an unauthorized transaction. For example, all employees should be on an electronic valid database. Any attempt to pay an employee not on the valid list should be rejected, and only attempts to pay valid employees should be accepted. Any attempt to pay an invalid employee should generate an exception report. Either the employee doesn't exist at all, or he or she is simply no longer working for the company.

356. (B) The total hours worked, 146, would be a batch total. Payroll is run in a batch, and the batch total would be the total hours worked during the period, which is represented as the total of column 2.

357. (A) The record count is five, as there are five paychecks or five employees to pay.

358. (B) A hash total attempts to detect if numbers that are not normally added (such as Social Security numbers or employee ID #s) have been processed incorrectly. An example of a hash total is the sum of the fifth digit of all employees' Social Security numbers. This amount is already predetermined and can function as a control that no employees have been added to the system.

359. (C) I and II are correct. Passwords are electronic access controls that authenticate user access to a system and its applications and data. A firewall is an electronic access control that prevents unauthorized access to a system and its applications and data.

360. (C) A cold site is an off-site location that has all the electrical connections and other physical requirements for data processing but does not have the actual hardware or software. (A) is wrong. A warm site may contain some or all of the hardware found in the original computer center but is not set up to function as an immediate backup center. (B) is wrong. A hot site will have hardware already installed at the alternate site. This hardware resembles the hardware at the original computer center and is already configured, or can be configured, to be the same as the company is using in its normal operations. (D) is wrong. The term *purple site* does not exist.

361. (D) I, II, and III are correct. Hot sites typically involve external providers of floor space and equipment, off premises, because in the event of certain disasters, the company's own space may be unavailable. Since all the equipment is there, the company simply provides its own application software and can be up and running in a very short time, often one to three hours.

362. (B) Intranets can be thought of as private, company-owned Internets. While the same web browser can be used for both the Internet and an intranet, intranets are privately sponsored forms of electronic data sharing normally used for organizational communications, not for public display. (A) is wrong. While the Internet is a public information highway, intranets tend to be private. (C) is wrong. A database management system is software that is in charge of providing data from a database to an application program and writing it back to disk. (D) is wrong. A compiler is a language processor, software that translates source code (human readable) to object code (machine readable).

Chapter 5: Economics

363. (B) II is correct. Gross domestic product (GDP) includes all final goods and services produced by resources within a country regardless of who owns the resources. Final US GDP would include output from a car factory in Detroit whether it's a factory owned by a US car company or a factory owned by a Japanese car company. I is wrong. GDP includes all final goods and services. Used goods that are resold would be excluded from GDP because they were already counted once when they were final.

364. (A) I is correct. Real gross domestic product (GDP) measures the value of all goods and services produced within a nation's borders in constant dollars. Real GDP is adjusted to account for changes in the price level and removes the effect of inflation by using a price index. Real GDP can be used to compare economic performance over time; nominal GDP cannot be used for that purpose because nominal GDP doesn't adjust for inflation. II is wrong. Nominal GDP is unadjusted for inflation. Nominal GDP measures the value of all final goods and services in current prices; therefore, it is not the best measure of economic performance.

365. (D) Economic activity is characterized by fluctuations, which vary in severity and duration. Severity refers to how deep a recession is or how widespread a recovery may be. Duration refers to time—how many quarters a recession lasts or how many years of growth until inflation.

366. (D) The peak marks the end of the expansionary phase and the beginning of the contraction phase. In the peak, firms are likely to face input shortages, leading to higher overall costs, and as a result of higher costs, profits begin to fall.

367. (D) During a recovery phase, economic activity begins to increase and return to its long-term growth trend. Demands for goods and services begin to rise, and company profits, no longer falling, begin to stabilize. (A) is wrong. A peak is the high point of economic activity and marks the end of expansion and the beginning of the contraction phase. At a peak, profits are at their highest level. (B) is wrong. Firm profits are likely to be falling during contraction, not stabilizing. (C) is wrong. During expansion, economic activity is rising beyond its average long-term growth trend.

368. (B) A trough is a low point of economic activity. Firm profits are at their lowest level, so cost cutting is essential for survival. Since jobs have been cut, demand for products is low and excess capacity would be expected.

369. (A) I is correct. During a recession, potential output will exceed actual output. II is wrong. During a recession, prices are falling, employment is low, and real gross domestic product is falling.

370. (B) II and III are correct. In a recession, gross domestic product (GDP) falls as unemployment rises. Rising unemployment and falling GDP are evidence of a recession. I is wrong. An increase in aggregate demand is not evidence of a recession. In a recession, GDP will fall if unemployment rises and there is a decrease in aggregate demand or a decrease in aggregate supply.

371. (C) Increasing government purchases (government spending) will cause an increase in demand. An increase in demand causes real gross domestic product (GDP) to rise and unemployment to fall. (B) is wrong. Decreasing taxes, rather than increasing taxes, will cause real GDP to rise. Increasing taxes will cause GDP to fall.

372. (D) I and II are wrong. Increasing taxes is an example of contracting rather than expansionary fiscal policy. A decrease in government spending is also an example of contracting fiscal policy rather than expansionary fiscal policy. Expansionary fiscal policy involves increasing government purchases and/or decreasing taxes. Expansionary fiscal policy would cause real gross domestic product (output) to increase.

373. (C) An increase in wealth and an increase in the general level of confidence shifts the aggregate demand curve to the right. Shifts in the aggregate demand curve occur due to factors other than price. Prices would cause a change in the quantity demanded along the same aggregate demand curve, but price would not be enough to cause a shift in the curve. A shift to the right (good news) would occur as a result of reasons other than price, including factors such as increases in wealth (stock market gains), reductions in interest rates, and increases in consumer confidence. (A) is wrong. An increase in wealth and an increase in overall confidence about the economic outlook does not increase the cost of capital.

374. (C) I and II are correct. As aggregate demand rises, output is up, gross domestic product (GDP) is up, and the employment rate goes up, which means unemployment decreases.

375. (C) I and II are correct. The aggregate demand curve is downward sloping because quantity demanded (QD) is inversely related to the price level. For example, as prices rise, QD falls. Slope is a measure of sensitivity—in this case, sensitivity of the dependent variable (quantity demanded) to the change in the independent variable, price level. The short-run aggregate supply curve is upward sloping because quantity supplied is directly related to the price level. In the short run, if prices rise, sellers will want to sell more (a positive slope). In this case, slope is measuring the sensitivity of the dependent variable (quantity supplied) to the change in the independent variable, price. Note that in the long run, the aggregate supply curve is not about price but about resources available such as labor, materials, and capital.

376. (B) II and III are correct. A nation's long-term aggregate supply curve represents the potential output of a nation, and long-run output is dependent on infrastructure, including available technology, capital, labor, and raw materials within the country. I is wrong. A nation's long-run aggregate supply curve is *not* dependent upon price levels; only the short-run aggregate supply curve is dependent upon price levels.

377. (A) If a company's input costs go down, the company could make more money by increasing production. When supply goes up, output goes up and gross domestic product (GDP) goes up. When supply goes up, price per unit will go down. Therefore, a decrease in input costs like direct material and direct labor would shift the aggregate supply curve to the right, resulting in an increase in real GDP and a decrease in the overall price level.

378. (C) I and II are correct. Real gross domestic product (GDP) per capita is typically used to compare standards of living across countries. Real GDP per capita is real GDP divided by population. By dividing real GDP by population, this measure adjusts for differences in the size of countries and differences in sizes of population over a period of time.

379. (B) II is correct. If the US dollar falls in value, the supply of foreign goods in the United States should decrease as imports become more expensive due to a falling dollar's not being able to purchase as much overseas. I is wrong. If the dollar falls in value, net exports will gain as US goods become less expensive overseas.

380. (A) I is correct. Inflation erodes purchasing power. II is wrong. Inflation actually helps anyone that has to make a fixed payment. While those making a fixed payment are helped, inflation hurts those who are receiving that same fixed payment.

381. (A) I is correct. Note the question asks what inflation does *not* do. I is right because inflation does not help those on a fixed income. It actually hurts those on a fixed income but helps those with a fixed obligation. II is wrong because it's a true statement. Inflation will increase the price level.

382. (A) An increase in aggregate demand causes output to rise and the price level to rise. If there are many buyers, price levels and output will rise, which will cause gross domestic product (GDP) and employment to rise. *Alternatively,* if there were few buyers, a decrease in aggregate demand would cause output to fall and the price level to fall.

383. (D) A decrease in aggregate supply causes output to fall and the price level to rise. A decrease in aggregate supply will lead to fewer goods being created, which could lead to shortages. If goods are scarce, the price will rise. Alternatively, an increase in aggregate supply would cause output to rise and the price level to fall, since more goods are being created. More goods created could lead to a surplus, which leads to lower prices.

384. (A) A mismatch of skills and jobs in the economy is an example of structural unemployment. (B) is wrong. Cyclical unemployment is caused by business cycles. Cyclical unemployment tends to rise during a recession and fall during an expansion. (C) is wrong. Frictional unemployment is a term for the time lag that individuals experience between jobs. (D) is wrong. Seasonal unemployment is caused by seasonal demand for labor.

385. (C) Cyclical unemployment is caused by business cycles. Cyclical unemployment tends to rise during a recession and fall during an expansion. (A) is wrong. Frictional unemployment is a term for the time lag that individuals experience between jobs. (B) is wrong. Structural unemployment is caused by a mismatch of skills and jobs in the economy. (D) is wrong. Seasonal unemployment is caused by seasonal demand for labor.

386. (B) If a new invention renders an entire industry obsolete, this leads to structural unemployment. When an industry is rendered obsolete, the labor that had been working in that industry needs to be retrained before those workers can be matched to a new industry.

387. (B) I and II are correct. Gross domestic product can be calculated using the expenditures approach or the income approach. III is wrong. There is no such thing as the net assets approach.

388. (C) I and II are correct. The expenditures approach to calculating gross domestic product includes:

Net exports
Capital investment
Consumption
Government expenditures

389. (B) II is correct. Business profits and employee compensation are used in the income approach for computing gross domestic product (GDP). The income approach follows the acronym PRIDE:

Profits to corporations and small business
Rental income
Interest income
Depreciation
Employee pay (wages)

I is wrong. The expenditures approach does not use business profits and employee compensation. The expenditures approach to calculating GDP is as follows:

Investment—capital investment by private business
Consumption—consumer spending
Exports—net of imports
Government expenditures

390. (D) The discount rate is set by the Federal Reserve and refers to the interest rate established for short-term (often overnight) loans the central bank makes to member banks.

391. (B) The gross domestic product (GDP), using the expenditures approach, is calculated as follows (all numbers are in the billions):

Government spending	$12
Net exports	+ $3*
Investments	+ $30
Consumption	+ $16
GDP—Expenditures approach	$61

392. (B) The gross domestic product (GDP) of **$606 billion** is calculated as follows:

Profits to proprietors	$83 billion
Profits to corporations	+ $119 billion
Rental income	+ $19 billion
Interest income	+ $80 billion
Depreciation†	
Employee wages	+ $305 billion
GDP—Income approach	$606 billion

Consumer spending and net imports would only be used under the expenditures approach.

---

*Exports of $7 less imports of $4 equals net exports of $3.
†Not applicable in this question, but Depreciation is part of the PRIDE acronym.

393. (D) Gross national product (GNP) is the sum of all final goods and services produced by residents of Pradera whether produced within Pradera's borders or produced by Pradera residents working outside Pradera's borders. (A) is wrong. Gross domestic product measures the value of all final goods and services produced within Pradera's borders whether produced by Pradera residents or produced by foreigners working in Pradera. (B) is wrong. Net domestic product is equal to GDP minus depreciation. (C) is wrong. Net national product is equal to GNP less economic depreciation. Economic depreciation measures the losses in the value of capital goods due to age and wear.

394. (D) The inflation rate measures the rate of increase in the overall price level in the economy. (A) is wrong. The prime rate is an interest rate charged by banks to their best credit risk borrowers. (B) is wrong. The discount rate is set by the Federal Reserve and refers to the interest rate established for short-term (often overnight) loans it makes to member banks. (C) is wrong. The nominal rate (of GDP) measures the level of economic output without taking into account the overall price level or inflation rate.

395. (C) The consumer price index (CPI) is primarily used to compare relative price changes over time. The CPI is a measure of the overall cost of a fixed basket of goods and services purchased by an average urban household.

396. (B) The annual inflation rate is calculated as follows:
$$133.5 - 121 = 12.5$$
$$12.5 \div 121 = 10.33\%$$

397. (A) The consumer price index is measured monthly and represents prices paid for a representative basket of goods and services.

398. (C) I and II are correct. Reserve requirements relate to how much money banks must keep in reserve rather than loan out to customers. The Federal Reserve can raise a bank's reserve requirements or lower it. Raising the reserve requirement dampens the economy; lowering the reserve requirement stimulates the economy. The Federal Reserve would most likely purchase government securities if the goal were to stimulate the economy. Purchasing these securities increases the money supply and expands the economy. On the other hand, were the Federal Reserve to sell government securities, this would take money out of the economy.

399. (C) I and III are correct. Reducing the discount rate will make it easier and cheaper to borrow and will expand the supply of money and stimulate the economy. When interest rates fall, aggregate demand increases and real gross domestic product increases—the economy grows! Purchasing of government securities by the Federal Reserve puts more money into the market and stimulates the economy. II is wrong. Increasing reserve requirements makes it harder for banks to lend, since banks would be forced to keep more on reserve. This contracts the supply of money and slows the economy.

400. (A) When the Federal Reserve has an expansionary monetary policy, interest rates fall, which stimulates the desired levels of business investment and personal and household consumption. Increases in desired investment and consumption cause an increase in aggregate demand and in gross domestic product.

401. (A) Precious metals are nonmonetary assets whose values increase with inflation. (B) and (C) are wrong. Bonds pay a fixed income to the investor, and fixed incomes suffer the most during a period of rising interest rates. (D) is wrong. As interest rates rise, the dividends and earnings may not keep up with inflation, making precious metals like gold and silver a better investment than common stock if inflation is expected.

402. (A) I is correct. In a perfectly competitive marketplace, customers are indifferent about which firm they buy from and will buy from the cheapest firm. II is wrong. In a perfectly competitive market, the level of a firm's output is small (not large) relative to the industry's total output. The lawn-cutting industry is a good example of a perfectly competitive market. With no brand loyalty, customers would switch based solely on price. Firms would not be able to charge more than the competition or they would lose sales.

403. (C) III is correct. In monopolistic competition, there are many firms, each with a slightly different product (product differentiation). I is wrong. In monopolistic competition, there are many firms. II is wrong. In monopolistic competition, there are relatively small or no barriers to entry. The fast-food industry is an example of monopolistic competition.

404. (C) I and II are correct. Firms produce up to the point where marginal cost equals marginal revenue, whether the markets are perfectly competitive or imperfectly competitive. In any industry, expanding production will increase profits up to the point that marginal revenue equals marginal cost. Marginal revenue is the additional revenue generated from selling one more unit of product. Marginal cost is the additional cost generated from producing one more unit. Regardless of the industry, firms will produce up to the point where marginal revenue equals marginal cost.

405. (A) II is correct. Oligopoly market conditions are characterized by the following:

Few firms in the market
Significant barriers to entry
Little or no variability in pricing

The international oil industry is an example of an oligopoly. It is run by OPEC and there are significant costs to compete, few firms, and so on. In an oligopoly, the other firms in the market will match any price reduction so they do not lose market share, but they will not automatically match a price increase of an individual firm. Therefore, the demand curve is said to be "kinked" for a firm competing in an oligopoly. I is wrong. Monopolistic competition involves many firms, few barriers to entry, and at least some differentiation among competitors' products. III is wrong. In perfect competition, there are many competitors, there are no real barriers to entry, and customers have no real preference about which firm they buy from.

406. (C) Elasticity of demand or supply is a measure of how sensitive the demand for or the supply of a product is to a change in its price. (A) is wrong. Marginal cost is defined as the total cost of producing one additional unit of output. (D) is wrong. The producer price index is another measure of inflation in addition to the consumer price index. (B) is wrong. Gross domestic product (GDP) is the most common measure of economic activity; it measures the total output of all final goods and services produced within a nation's borders over a particular time period.

407. (C) If demand is price inelastic, an increase in price will result in an increase in total revenue. An example of a product with inelastic demand is a Super Bowl ticket. A 10 percent increase in price would result in a decrease in demand of far less than 10 percent, so total revenue would increase as a result of an increase in price. This is probably why Super Bowl tickets increase in price by at least 10 percent every year.

408. (B) II is correct. When demand is elastic, an increase in price will result in an overall drop in total revenue rather than an increase in revenue, possibly as a result of many substitutes for product G being available in the marketplace. Although Poplar is raising its price, if there were many substitutes available for product G, quantity demanded would be more sensitive to a price increase, and therefore total revenue would decrease. I is wrong. Demand for product G is elastic rather than inelastic. Demand for product G is sensitive because a 20 percent increase in price results in a 30 percent decrease in units sold. A 30 percent decrease in quantity demanded divided by a 20 percent increase in price equals 1.5. Any result greater than 1 positive or negative means the demand is elastic. The higher the number greater than 1 (absolute value), the more sensitive the product is to a price increase. In this case, quantity demanded for product G is sensitive to a price increase.

409. (D) I and II are wrong. When demand for a product is unit elastic, elasticity is equal to 1. Any price change would be offset by an equal change in demand, so a price increase would be offset by an equal drop in demand, resulting in no change in total revenue. In addition, when demand for a product is unit elastic, elasticity is equal to 1. Any price change would be offset by an equal change in demand, so a price decrease would be offset by an equal increase in demand, resulting in no change in total revenue.

410. (A) Supply is price inelastic if the absolute price elasticity of supply is less than 1. (B), (C), and (D) are wrong. If the absolute price elasticity of supply is greater than 1, supply is elastic, rather than inelastic. Supply is unit elastic if the absolute price elasticity is equal to 1. Price elasticity of supply is determined by dividing change in quantity supplied by change in price. Any number greater than 1 is said to be supply price elastic and more sensitive to a change in price. As price goes up, quantity supplied should go up, but the question is by how much. If a firm has idle capacity, it would be willing and able to produce more as output prices rise, but if it were already at full capacity, the higher selling price would have less of an impact.

411. (D) If the elasticity of demand for a normal good is estimated to be 1.23, then a 10 percent increase in its price would cause a decrease in quantity demanded of 12.3 percent (10% × 1.23 elasticity of demand = 12.3%). If price rises, quantity demanded falls, and in this case, total revenue would fall since demand for this item is sensitive to a price increase because the estimated elasticity is 1.23 (greater than 1). Any number greater than 1 is considered more sensitive to a price change. As quantity demanded falls, revenue falls. In this case, revenue would drop by 12.3 percent along with quantity demanded.

412. (D) In a value chain, value starts with the suppliers who provide the raw materials for a production process, continues with the firm, continues with the value created by the customers, and then ends with the disposal and recycling of the materials.

413. (B) I and II are correct. Factors that increase the bargaining power of the customer include awareness by customers that they make up a large volume of a firm's business. Such awareness gives customers the power to dominate negotiations. More information available about dealer costs and substitute products in the marketplace gives customers increased bargaining power as well. III is wrong. A low, rather than high, switching cost would give customers more bargaining power.

414. (C) I and II are correct. Competitive advantage is generally defined as either differentiation or cost leadership. Differentiation advantage may be best obtained by a firm that builds market share or increases its price. A firm enjoys a competitive advantage as a cost leader when it's able to match the prices of its rivals or has a cost structure that is lower than its competition.

415. (B) II is correct. Brand loyalty will cause cost leadership strategies to fail. If customers are loyal to a particular brand, a price decrease by a competitor would be offset by brand loyalty. The best cost strategy is a combination of the benefits of cost leadership and differentiation strategies.

416. (A) I and II are correct. The supply chain operations reference (SCOR) model includes a series of processes or steps defined as **plan, source, make,** and **deliver**. The process of planning consists of developing a way to properly balance aggregate demand and aggregate supply within the goals and objectives of the firm and then plan for the necessary infrastructure. II is correct. The "deliver" process encompasses all the activities of getting the finished product into the hands of the ultimate consumers. III is wrong. Record is *not* part of the SCOR model. The SCOR model can be described as follows: **Planning** is the first step. Try to forecast demand because a firm doesn't want to overproduce or underproduce and needs to know what to purchase in terms of materials. **Sourcing** deals with where the firm is going to get the materials needed for production. Sourcing includes selecting vendors and paying vendors. The **make** stage of SCOR is where the conversion costs are added—the labor and overhead. The result of the make stage is that the final product is completed. The **deliver** stage means shipping the final product to the customer.

417. (B) Selecting vendors is a source decision. (A) is wrong. Planning relates to the necessary infrastructure needed to properly balance aggregate demand and aggregate supply within the goals and objectives of the firm. (C) is wrong. The deliver stage includes all the activities related to getting the finished product into the hands of the ultimate consumers. (D) is wrong. The make stage refers to production sites and methods.

418. (C) II is correct. The fundamental law of demand holds that there is an inverse relationship between price of the product and the quantity demanded. If the price of A goes up, the quantity demanded for A should fall. I is wrong. If A and B are true substitutes and the price of A rises, the quantity demanded of B should rise, not fall. III is wrong. If A and B are true substitutes, then if the price of A rises, demand for B should rise as customers choose B. The price of A and the price of B are not necessarily related at all. An increase in the price of A does not result in an automatic increase in the price of B.

419. (B) If goods are substitutes, as the price of one goes up, the demand for the other increases as consumers seek the lower-priced substitute good. (A) is wrong. Complementary goods move together; as the price of steak goes up, the demand for steak sauce drops. (C) is wrong. Independent goods have no relationship; as the price of wood increases, the demand for laundry detergent is not impacted. (D) is wrong. Demand for inferior (low-end) goods declines as wages increase.

420. (B) If supply decreases, the product becomes scarce and prices will increase. If quantity demanded for a product goes up, this drives price up also.

421. (C) I and II are correct. The elasticity of demand for a good is calculated by measuring the change in quantity demanded over the change in price. The elasticity of demand for a normal good is always negative—as prices rise, demand falls. The demand for normal goods will increase as income rises.

422. (A) I is correct. If demand is inelastic, few good substitutes are available for the product. NFL play-off and Super Bowl tickets are inelastic because there are few if any substitutes for these products. Those who want to see the games in person will pay. A ticket price increase will bring additional revenue. II is wrong. If demand is inelastic, a decline in price will not result in an increase in total revenue. Instead, if demand is inelastic, a decline in price would lead to a decrease in total revenue.

423. (A) Price elasticity of demand is calculated by dividing the percentage change in quantity demanded by the percentage change in price, using the average values of both.

Step 1—Divide change in quantity by average quantity.
$(40,000 - 60,000) \div 50,000 = -20,000 \div 50,000 = -0.4$

Step 2—Divide change in price by average price.
$\$5 \div \$27.50 = 0.1818$

Step 3—Divide change in quantity by change in price.
$-0.4 \div 0.1818 = -2.20$

Any number greater than 1 (in absolute terms) indicates elastic demand rather than inelastic demand. This means that although the result is negative, -2.20, rather than 2.20, any number greater than 1 indicates elastic demand rather than inelastic demand.

424. (C) When a good is demanded, no matter what the price, demand is described as perfectly inelastic. A newborn baby requiring milk and formula is an example of perfectly inelastic demand. Insulin for diabetics is another example of perfectly inelastic demand.

425. (C) I and II are correct. Strengths and weaknesses focus on internal factors. Opportunities and threats relate to external factors. A SWOT analysis is the study of strengths, weaknesses, opportunities, and threats (SWOT). Evaluation of internal and external factors contributing to an organization's success is referred to as a SWOT analysis.

426. (A) Comparative advantage suggests that even if one of two regions is absolutely more efficient in the production of every good than is the other, if each region specializes in the products in which it has greatest relative efficiency, trade will be mutually profitable to both regions. Comparative advantage leads to globalization. A characteristic of globalization is increased specialization. (B) is wrong. With economies of scale, firms may experience increasing returns because they operate more efficiently. With growth may come specialization of labor and related production efficiencies that reduce average costs. (C) is wrong. With the law of diminishing returns, a firm gets too large in the short run and an increase in labor or capital beyond a certain point causes a less than proportionate increase in production. (D) is wrong. The high-low method enables managers to estimate variable and fixed costs based on the highest and lowest levels of activity during the period.

Chapter 6: Management of Risk

427. (D) In the long run, all factors of production are variable and the firm has the opportunity to change the factors of production, such as by expanding or contracting in response to changes in consumer demand. In the short run, that is not possible quickly enough and that is when the law of diminishing returns sets in. In the long run, firms may experience increasing returns because they operate more efficiently. With growth may come specialization of labor and related production efficiencies that reduce average costs. This increased efficiency is referred to as economies of scale. (A) and (B) are wrong. All costs are broken down between fixed and variable in the short run, not the long run. The short run is within the "relevant range." The relevant range assumes that all fixed costs will not change. Costs are only fixed for the short term; for example, eventually leases expire and either need to be renewed or are not renewed. (C) is wrong. Economies of scale are long-term advantages of production efficiencies. These advantages come from experience and are not possible in the short run due to the law of diminishing returns.

428. (B) I, II, and III are correct. Porter's five forces affecting a firm's performance are intensity of firm rivalry, threat of substitute goods, threat of new competitors, bargaining power of customers, and bargaining power of suppliers. Intensity of firm rivalry is the first and most important factor affecting a firm's performance. The intensity of rivalry depends on the other four factors. The threat of substitute goods limits a firm's pricing power since consumers will switch to another product if the price differential becomes too high. If entry into an industry is relatively easy, firms within the industry face competition from new entrants if prices become too high and excess profits are earned. If customers hold bargaining power, there is a limit to price increases. In addition, a firm's cost structure and profitability are affected by the bargaining power of suppliers.

429. (A) I and II are correct. Storage costs add no value to a firm, so a just in time system seeks to minimize storage costs, thus reducing nonvalue-added operations like storage. The just in time system focuses on expediting the production process by having materials available as needed without having to store them prior to usage. III is wrong. *Just in time* means that employees with multiple skills are used more efficiently and will not specialize in merely one job or task.

430. (C) I and II are correct. Conformance costs include prevention and appraisal. The term *conformity* describes goods that agree with manufacturing specifications. Conformance costs relate to investing a little extra money in the front end to make sure there are few or no problems later. The theory is that if a company spends a little extra on conformance, the result is a better-quality product and less failure. Prevention refers to training and preventive maintenance. Appraisal refers to inspection, and appraisal costs help discover and remove a defect before it's shipped to the customer or to the next department. Testing is an example of appraisal. Nonconformance costs include internal and external failures. The term *nonconformity* is a synonym for *failure*. The cost of failure is high, often resulting in lost customers and damaged reputation. Failure costs are referred to as nonconformance costs.

431. (B) I and III are correct. Maintenance of machinery and inspection of final product are conformance costs found under the category of prevention cost. The two categories of conformance cost are prevention and appraisal. Prevention includes maintenance of equipment and inspection. Appraisal includes testing and inspection. Conformance costs are incurred to minimize nonconformance. II is wrong. Repair is a nonconformance (failure) cost. It is an external failure cost. Failure (nonconformance) is expensive; the real price is often lost customers and damaged reputation. Therefore, the theory is that higher conformance costs should lead to lower nonconformance costs, or less failure.

432. (B) II is correct. There are external failure costs as well as internal failure costs. The question asked for an internal failure cost. Internal failure costs are discovered by the next department within the company rather than by the customer. When Department #2 sends back the product to Department #1 for rework and Department #1 needs to retool in order to do the rework, these are examples of internal failure costs. I is wrong. Product repair (warranty) is an external failure cost. When nonconforming products are detected by customers, the failure is considered external and warranty costs start to be incurred.

433. (D) I and II are wrong. Repair is an external failure cost, discovered by customers. When nonconformance (failure) is discovered by customers, the costs are considered external failure costs. Rework is an internal failure cost. When the nonconformance (failure) is discovered within the company, the costs are considered internal failure costs. Rework and repair are nonconformance costs.

434. (B) II is correct. Business process reengineering seeks radical change by ignoring the current process and instead starting from the beginning to design a different way of achieving the end goal and/or product. I is wrong. Business process management seeks incremental change by fine-tuning and tweaking the existing process and design. The advantage of incremental change (process management) is that if the change goes badly, the company is still left with a process that works.

435. (B) The project manager is responsible for project administration on a day-to-day basis, including identifying and managing internal and external stakeholder expectations. (A) is wrong. The project sponsor is the party ultimately responsible for the success or failure of the project. The project sponsor is a member of top management that secures the funding and resources for the project. The sponsor interfaces between the organization and the project team itself but does not manage the project daily. (C) is wrong. The steering committee has oversight but does not manage the project on a daily basis. The project sponsor is the chair of the steering committee, and the remainder of the steering committee may be from within or outside the organization. (D) is wrong. The project members carry out the work and produce the final output known as the product "deliverables," but they do not manage the project on a day-to-day basis.

436. (A) From top to bottom, the order is:

Board of Directors
↓
Steering Committee
↓
Project Sponsor
(has ultimate responsibility)
↓
Project Manager
↓
Project Members

Within project management, the project manager is supervised by the project sponsor. The project sponsor reports to the steering committee, and the steering committee reports to the board of directors.

437. (D) The project sponsor is responsible for overall project delivery and is an individual at the executive level of management. The project sponsor is also responsible for allocating funding and resources to the project. (B) is wrong. The project manager communicates project metrics to stakeholders and team members and manages the project daily but does not have responsibility for overall project delivery because some of the requirements to complete the project are outside the project manager's control. For example, funding for the project could be cut and the project manager would not be able to complete the project.

438. (A) I is correct. The project sponsor should communicate project needs to the executive steering committee, not to the board of directors. II is wrong. The project sponsor does not approach the board of directors. Instead, the steering committee will approach the board of directors if the project sponsor can first convince the steering committee that the project is in the best interest of the company.

439. (C) Globalization represents the increased dispersion and integration of the world's economies. It is often objectively measured as the growth in world trade as a percentage of gross domestic product. Globalization is frequently associated with comparative advantage and increased specialization.

440. (A) I is correct. Short-term financing has increased credit risk since financing has not been secured long term; there is an increased risk that credit will be denied once the short-term debt matures. II is wrong. Short-term financing typically results in lower cost than long-term financing. Lower costs translate into higher profits. Therefore, short-term financing results in higher profitability (not lower profitability) than long-term financing. The reason that long-term financing results in higher costs than short-term financing is the higher interest rate risk for the lender associated with fixed long-term rates. The lender wants to be compensated for assuming a fixed rate of interest for a longer period of time. Short-term financing has as its advantage lower cost of borrowing, thus increasing profitability. Disadvantages with short-term borrowing include increased interest rate risk since no long-term rate was locked in. Less potential credit available in the future is another disadvantage of short-term borrowing. Long-term financing involves securing a rate for longer periods of time. Long-term financing is more expensive than short-term financing, which results in lower profits, but long-term financing has as an advantage: less interest rate risk and less credit risk.

441. (C) I and II are correct. Diversifiable risk includes unique risk, firm-specific risk of that particular investment. Since the risk is firm specific, it can be diversified away in a portfolio of investments of different risks. II is also correct. Diversifiable risk includes unsystematic risk. Unsystematic risk has less to do with the system and more to do with the stock itself. Since the risk is more stock than stock market, it also can be diversified away in a portfolio of investments of different risks.

442. (B) The lender's default risk is based on the borrower's credit risk. Default risk impacts lenders. Lenders are exposed to default risk to the extent that it's possible that its borrowers will not repay the principal or interest due. Credit risk impacts borrowers. Exposure to credit risk includes a company's inability to secure financing or secure favorable credit terms as a result of poor credit ratings.

443. (B) Purchasing power risk is the risk that price levels will change and affect asset values (mostly real estate). (A) is wrong. Interest rate risk is the fluctuation in the value of a "financial asset" when interest rates change. (C) is wrong. Liquidity risk is associated with the ability to sell the temporary investment in a short period of time without significant price concessions. (D) is wrong. Financial risk is a general category of risk that includes default risk and interest rate risk along with purchasing power risk, market risk, and liquidity risk.

444. (C) If the market rate of interest increases, the value of the bond will decrease. This is true because the coupon rate is fixed, and if investors can do better elsewhere, the price of Wildwood Corporation bonds will drop.

445. (A) If the foreign currency depreciates, the domestic currency appreciates. Since the US company has net cash outflows, a drop in value of the foreign currency would benefit the US company because such a drop means a drop in liabilities to the US company. Any drop in liabilities is considered a positive.

446. (D) I and II are wrong. If the foreign currency appreciates and there are net cash inflows, that is positive for the US company because it will be paid in inflated dollars. If the foreign currency depreciates and the US company has net cash outflows, that's also positive for the US company because when the foreign currency depreciates, the domestic currency appreciates. If the foreign currency appreciates, the US company wants to have net cash inflows. Net cash outflows would be good if the foreign currency depreciates.

447. (C) II is correct. The decision to exercise a call option would *not* be based on the amount paid for the call premium. The amount paid for the call, the call premium, would represent a sunk cost. Sunk costs are *not* relevant in decision-making. I is wrong. The decision to exercise a call option would be based on the strike price. The strike price is the price at which the shares represented by the call options could be purchased. III is wrong. The decision to exercise a call option would be based on the market price of the stock. If the strike price were below market price, the options would likely be exercised. However, if the market price were below the strike price, the decision would likely be made to let the call options expire.

448. (D) Compared to US Treasury securities, equity securities and corporate bonds are both more risky. US Treasury securities are considered the least risky securities on the planet since they are backed by the full faith and credit of the US Treasury, which, so far, has never defaulted.

449. (A) A strong US dollar makes domestic goods relatively more expensive than imported goods. (B) is wrong. It is better for a US company when the value of the US dollar weakens, not strengthens, because a weak US dollar makes domestic goods relatively cheaper, compared to imported goods. (C) and (D) are wrong. A weak US dollar makes domestic goods relatively less expensive than imported goods.

450. (B) II is correct. When the price of the pound rises, the price of British goods will also increase, and the pound will buy the same amount of British goods but more US goods. I is wrong. If the price of the pound increases relative to the US dollar, it will buy the same amount of British goods, not more.

451. (B) II is correct. Having a foreign subsidiary subjects the domestic entity to foreign currency translation risk because when the US firm ultimately converts those financial statements from the Japanese currency back to the parent's currency, there could be big changes in amounts—especially if the local currency is not stable. I is wrong. No translation exposure exists since there is no foreign investment or foreign subsidiary. The US entity exporting goods to Canada would be subject to foreign currency transaction risk but not subject to foreign currency translation risk unless it makes an investment in a foreign entity or has a foreign subsidiary.

452. (A) I is correct. The premium for the put option is a sunk cost and is not relevant to the decision on whether to exercise the put option. II is wrong. The premium paid for the put option is relevant to determining the total amount of asset value preserved.

453. (A) Total interest for the loan is $100,000 × 0.06 = $6,000.

15% × $100,000 = $15,000 compensating balance
$85,000 net proceeds
$6,000 ÷ $85,000 = 7.05%

454. (B) II is correct. Business risk represents the risk associated with the unique circumstances of a particular company. For example, if Hayes Corporation attempted to capitalize its operations using only its cumulative earnings, this could affect shareholder value significantly if the economy were to take a downturn and business were to slow. Therefore, relying solely on earnings for sustainability and growth is known as business risk. I is wrong. If an entity uses only its own cumulative earnings in capitalizing its operations, it's *not* exposed to the risk of defaulting on loans, which is known as financial risk. III is wrong. If an entity uses only its own cumulative earnings, then it is neither borrowing nor lending, so it's not exposed to the risks that the value of its financial instruments will change as a result of changes in interest rates, which is known as interest rate risk.

455. (C) II and III are correct. Interest rate risk, otherwise known as maturity risk premium, is an appropriate risk adjustment to the risk-free rate of return and is the compensation investors demand for bearing risk. Maturity risk premium, or interest rate risk, increases with the term to maturity—the longer the term to maturity, the greater the maturity risk premium. I is wrong. Default risk premium, not interest rate risk, is an appropriate risk adjustment to the risk-free rate of return and is the additional compensation demanded by lenders for bearing the risk that the issuer of the security will fail to pay the interest or fail to repay the principal.

456. (C) The expected return is calculated by summing the outcomes weighted by their probability of occurrence:

$100,000 × 0.1	$10,000
$600,000 × 0.3	+ $180,000
$900,000 × 0.2	+ $180,000
$300,000 × 0.4	+ $120,000
Expected return	$490,000

457. (C) The sales volume is calculated as follows:

$5,000 \times 0.1$	500
$11,000 \times 0.4$	$+ 4,400$
$30,000 \times 0.3$	$+ 9,000$
$100,000 \times 0.2$	$+ \underline{20,000}$
Total	33,900 units

458. (D) I and II are wrong. A corporation about to issue new bonds agreeing to a debt covenant is generally good for potential bondholders and for the issuing corporation. It would probably reduce the coupon rate on the bonds being sold since the covenant generally serves to protect the bondholder's interests by placing restrictions on the issuing debtor. Such a covenant might raise, not lower, a company's bond rating because there would be less risk. A debt covenant is a provision in a bond indenture (contract between the bond issuer and the bondholders) that the bond issuer will refrain from doing what it otherwise has a legal right to do or possibly do something that it otherwise would not be required to do. Maintaining better than a 2:1 current ratio at all times is an example of a debt covenant. Violating a debt covenant would have consequences; for example, the entire debt could be due and payable immediately if the firm drops below the 2:1 current ratio. A debt covenant would normally increase the value of the bonds and lower the coupon rate due to decreased risk.

459. (A) The sale of bonds to raise capital involves an immediate increase in cash but requires specific fixed payments and increases debt. Issuing bonds increases the debt equity ratio. The sale of common stock to raise capital does not require any payment and does not mature, and, because it increases equity while having no effect on debt, it decreases the debt equity ratio.

460. (C) The P/E ratio is calculated in three parts:

Step 1—Subtract preferred dividend from net income (numerator).

Step 2—Calculate earnings per share (EPS).
(Net income − preferred dividend) ÷ # of shares outstanding = EPS

Step 3—Calculate P/E ratio.
Market price of the stock ÷ Earnings per share (calculated in step 2) = P/E ratio

(B) is wrong because it calculates EPS, not P/E ratio. (A) is wrong. Market price per share divided by net income is not how the P/E ratio is calculated. (D) is wrong. Market price per share at the beginning of the year less market price per share at year-end is not how the P/E ratio is calculated.

461. (A) I is correct. The P/E ratio measures the amount that investors are willing to pay for each dollar of earnings per share. II is wrong. Higher P/E ratios generally indicate that investors are anticipating more growth and are bidding up the price of the shares in advance of performance.

462. (B) The P/E multiple is calculated as follows:

K = Required rate of 11 percent
G = Forecasted growth rate of 9 percent
The estimated P/E multiple = Payout ÷ (K − G)
$0.3 \div (0.11 - 0.09)$
$= 0.3 \div 0.02 = 15\times$

463. (B) II is correct. Debt security holders receive a periodic interest payment, while equity security holders only receive income when dividends are declared at the discretion of the board of directors.

464. (B) II is correct. The constant growth model assumes that the growth rate is less than the discount rate. I is wrong. An underlying assumption of the constant growth model is the idea that the stock price will grow at the same rate as the dividend, thereby producing a constant growth rate.

465. (A) The share price is calculated as follows:

Dividend ÷ desired return
$4 ÷ 10% = $40

The stock should sell for $40 per share to return 10 percent because $40 × 0.1 = $4 dividend per share. A zero growth model assumes that the next dividend is equal to the current dividend.

466. (D) The price an investor is willing to pay today does not depend on what the dividend is today but on what the dividend is likely to be one year from now. The growth rate is 5 percent, so take today's $4 dividend and multiply by 1.05. Next year's dividend is expected to be $4.20; $4.20, next year's dividend, is the numerator. The denominator is the required rate of return, 20 percent minus the growth rate of 5 percent, so 15 percent is the denominator. Therefore, an investor is willing to pay for this stock today: $4.20 ÷ 0.15 = $28 per share. Common stock is valued based on next year's dividend; preferred stock is based on a dividend that is fixed. Common stock is valued based on growing dividends, while preferred stockholders receive a fixed dividend.

467. (B) The P/E ratio is 20; therefore, the price is equal to the price divided by earnings anticipated for the coming year:

Price ÷ $18 = 20
Price = $360

468. (B) II is correct. Confirmation bias occurs when managers use data that confirm their conclusions and ignore data that challenge their ideas. I is wrong. A manager's belief that results will generally be positive is called excessive optimism, not confirmation bias.

469. (B) II is correct. The P/E ratio uses sales per share as a basis for valuation and can be used in start-up situations or under conditions where earnings data are not meaningful. Net sales, rather than net income, would be the numerator and total shares outstanding would be the denominator. I is wrong. If the company has regular earnings, earnings per share rather than sales per share would be a more meaningful expression of performance.

470. (A) I is correct. The P/E ratio is not meaningful if earnings are extremely small or if there is a loss. By name, the P/E ratio implies that there are earnings. Without sufficient earnings, the P/E ratio could not be used to determine a valuation of the company, whether the stock is selling for a fair price. Therefore, without sufficient earnings, the P/E ratio would not be used and a different measure of valuation like price to sales might be used instead. II is wrong. Price to sales ratio projection approaches can provide meaningful information in the event that net earnings are negative because even an entity with zero earnings still may command a certain valuation, especially if sales are expected to grow exponentially, which may generate the anticipation of profits.

471. (C) III is correct. Financial managers that believe their actions will cause earnings to increase and impact the marketplace are suffering from an illusion of control. I is wrong. Confirmation bias occurs when managers use data that confirm their conclusions and ignore data that challenge their ideas. II is wrong. Excessive optimism is a manager's belief that results will generally be positive.

Chapter 7: Corporate Governance

472. (A) I is correct. The Sarbanes-Oxley Act requires public companies to establish an audit committee that is directly responsible for the appointment, compensation, and oversight of the auditor. II is wrong. An annual audit provides meaningful information about financial reporting but does not address the issue of board oversight.

473. (C) I and II are correct. The CEO and CFO sign certain representations regarding annual and quarterly reports.

474. (C) I and II are correct. The CEO and CFO must assert that they have reviewed the annual report and that there are no untrue statements and that no material information has been omitted.

475. (A) I is correct. Enhanced financial disclosures include contingent obligations such as pending lawsuits where the loss has not been accrued. II is wrong. In consolidated financial statements, related party transactions are eliminated, so they would not affect the financial statements.

476. (D) I, II, and III are correct. All correcting adjustments noted by the independent auditor need to be disclosed as an enhanced disclosure. In addition, with unconsolidated financial statements (equity method), related party transactions should be fully disclosed. Disclosures would put the readers on notice of the relationship because it increases the risk of investing in the company. Finally, enhanced disclosures include off–balance sheet financing. All material off–balance sheet financing transactions like operating leases must be disclosed.

477. (C) I and II are correct. The Sarbanes-Oxley Act requires that the management report on internal control include management's assumption of responsibility for internal control. The act also requires that the management report on internal control include management's assessment of internal control effectiveness.

478. (B) II is correct. The Sarbanes-Oxley Act requires that the management report on internal control include a statement that the independent auditor has attested and reported on management's evaluation of internal controls. I is wrong. Management does not describe disagreements, if any, between management and the auditor. Under the act, financial statement disclosures include management's assumption of responsibility for internal control, management's assessment of internal control effectiveness, and a statement that the auditor has reported on management's evaluation of internal control.

479. (C) I and II are correct. The act specifically requires that the code of ethics include provisions for full, fair, accurate, and timely disclosure in periodic financial statements and that the code of ethics include provisions for honest and ethical conduct.

480. (D) I and II are wrong. The partner in charge of the audit firm engaged to do the audit should not be the financial expert on the audit committee. Under the Sarbanes-Oxley Act, one member of the audit committee needs to be named the financial expert. However, no real hard rules for who must be named the financial expert exist under the act.

481. (A) I is correct. The Sarbanes-Oxley Act requires that an issuer's audit committee have at least one financial expert or disclose why that role is not filled. II is wrong. Under the act, one member of the audit committee needs to be designated the financial expert. However, no real hard rules for who must be named the financial expert exist. The level of experience and training required of the financial expert is left up to the audit committee.

482. (C) I and II are correct. The board of directors would likely evaluate qualifications to serve on the audit committee and would likely evaluate qualifications needed to be designated the financial expert based on mix of knowledge and experience. The Sarbanes-Oxley Act is silent as to what group has the authority to designate an individual a financial expert but, in practice, the board of directors most often makes that decision.

483. (C) I and II are correct. According to the Committee of Sponsoring Organizations (COSO), within the control environment, management's operating style relates to work ethic and to a general overall commitment to effective financial reporting. The COSO framework is considered the standard for assessing good internal control over financial reporting. The COSO framework is the result of the Treadway Commission back in 1992 to develop best practices in the area of internal control.

484. (D) I and II are wrong. While achieving a CPA certificate is an outstanding personal accomplishment, it would not automatically qualify an individual to serve as an audit committee financial expert. While a full-time tenured professor of accounting at a major university with a PhD would be expected to know the GAAP rules, this would not automatically qualify the individual to serve as an audit committee financial expert. The Sarbanes-Oxley Act does not provide any guidance on who would automatically qualify to serve as financial expert. Someone with academic success may still lack the experience needed to be a financial expert on an audit engagement. Audit committee members should use their judgment in all cases to determine who would qualify.

485. (D) I and II are wrong. Within the Committee of Sponsoring Organizations (COSO) framework of control environment, recruitment of employees is a human resources function, as is retention and evaluation of employees. Within the COSO framework of control environment, management's operating style relates more to work ethic and commitment to effective financial reporting than employee recruitment, retention, and evaluation. The regular evaluation of employees for their competence in financial reporting is a human resources function as it relates to policies and achieving financial reporting objectives.

486. (A) I is correct. The regular evaluation of employees for their competence in financial reporting is an important link between human resources policies and the achievement of financial reporting objectives. II is wrong. Management's operating style relates more to work ethic and commitment to effective financial reporting than the recruitment, retention, and evaluation of employees.

487. (A) I is correct. The existence of a published code of ethics and a periodic acknowledgment that ethical values are understood is evidence of a development of ethical values and a commitment to ensuring that those values are understood and taken seriously. II is wrong. Board oversight relates more to overall leadership than to the specifics of ethical behavior.

488. (A) I is correct. The existence of a compliance program that includes both ethics training and a hotline for anonymous reporting is evidence of the development of ethical values and ensuring that those values are understood and taken seriously. II is wrong. Appropriate delegation relates to the organization's assignment of duties rather than to the specifics of ethical behavior.

489. (A) I is correct. Active engagement by an audit committee in representing the board of directors relative to all matters of internal and external audits is evidence of the board's understanding of its oversight responsibility over financial reporting. II is wrong. The organizational structure principle typically involves the appropriate alignment of reporting relationships to ensure that controls are not undermined (e.g., internal auditors should not report to the CFO but rather to the audit committee).

490. (D) External communications anticipate that matters affecting the achievement of financial reporting are communicated with outside parties. (A) is wrong. Internal control information is needed to facilitate the function of control components and is identified, captured, used, and distributed in a timely manner that enables personnel to fulfill their responsibilities. Reporting that triggers prompt exception resolution, root cause analysis, and control updates illustrates this principle. (B) is wrong. Internal communications anticipate that communications enable and support understanding and execution of internal control objectives, processes, and individual responsibilities. (C) is wrong. Variance analysis specifically supports internal control, not communications generally.

491. (A) Variance analysis specifically supports internal control information, not financial reporting, internal communications, or external communications generally.

492. (A) According to the Committee of Sponsoring Organizations of the Treadway Commission, reporting that triggers prompt exception resolution, root cause analysis, and control updates illustrates the principle of internal control information. Internal control information is needed to facilitate the function of control components in a timely manner that enables personnel to fulfill their responsibilities. (B) is wrong. Financial reporting information principles anticipate that information is identified, captured, used at all levels of the company, and distributed in a manner that supports the achievement of financial reporting objectives. (C) is wrong. Internal communications anticipate that communications enable and support understanding and execution of internal control objectives, processes, and individual responsibilities. (D) is wrong. External communications anticipate that matters affecting the achievement of financial reporting are communicated with outside parties.

493. (B) II is correct. The monitoring component of the integrated framework includes the principle that deficiencies should be timely identified, reported, and investigated in ongoing and separate evaluations. I is wrong. The control environment component includes the tone at the top and ethics.

494. (B) According to the COSO framework, risk assessments involve the determination of the likelihood and impact of events on the achievement of objectives. (A) is wrong. Control activities are the methods used to implement the response to risk. Sometimes the control activity is also, effectively, the risk response. (C) is wrong. Inherent risk is the risk to an entity in the absence of any actions management might take to alter either the risk's likelihood or impact. Risk responses are developed to deal with inherent risk. (D) is wrong. Residual risk is the risk that still remains after management responds to the risk and the control activities are in place.

495. (C) A response to risk that involves the diversification of product offerings rather than the elimination of product offerings is called risk reduction.

496. (D) Insuring against losses or entering into joint ventures to address risk is known as risk sharing.

497. (D) I and II are correct. According to the Committee of Sponsoring Organizations (COSO), maintaining adequate staffing to keep overtime and benefit costs within budget is an operational objective. In addition, maintaining direct labor cost variances within published guidelines is an operational objective. III is wrong. According to COSO, maintaining accounting principles that conform to US GAAP is a reporting objective rather than an operational objective.

498. (A) I is correct. The control activities component of the enterprise risk management (ERM) framework includes key elements that relate to the policies and procedures that ensure appropriate responses to identified risks, not to ethical values. II is wrong. The internal environment component (rather than the control activities component) of the ERM framework includes foundational elements such as organizational structure, assignment of authority and responsibility, integrity and ethical values, risk management philosophy, commitment to competence and human resources standards, and similar issues that influence the tone of the organization.

499. (A) I is correct. The commitment to ethical behavior begins with the tone at the top and is best established by management's demonstrated commitment to ethical behavior. II is wrong. The monitoring component or function of the internal control framework (rather than the tone at the top) is designed to ensure that internal controls continue to operate effectively. Monitoring is often left to the internal auditors, not to top management.

500. (D) I and II are correct. The International Professional Practices Framework organizes the authoritative guidance published by the Institute of Internal Auditors into two categories: mandatory guidance and endorsed/strongly recommended guidance. III is wrong. There is no such category as guidance currently under consideration.

Bonus Questions

501. (C) I and II are correct. The International Standards for the Professional Practice of Internal Auditing is considered mandatory, as is the code of ethics, which applies to individuals and entities that perform internal audits. Also considered mandatory is the International Professional Practices Framework definition of internal auditing.

502. (B) I and II are correct. The International Professional Practices Framework strongly recommends (but does *not* mandate) practice guides and position papers. III is wrong. The code of ethics issued by the IPPF is mandatory.

503. (A) The code of ethics, issued as part of the International Professional Practices Framework (IPPF) for internal auditing, provides principles and rules of conduct under four headings:

Integrity
Objectivity
Confidentiality
Competency

504. (B) According to the code of ethics, an internal auditor must refrain from assessing specific operations for which he or she was responsible within the previous year. Objectivity is presumed to be impaired if an internal auditor provides assurance services for an activity for which the internal auditor had responsibility within the previous year.

505. (C) According to COSO, a company's internal controls are measured by five inter-related components, which include the control environment, risk assessment, information and communication, control activities, and monitoring. The control environment reflects the overall tone of the organization and its commitment to effective financial reporting. Risk assessment allows management to identify risk and take action to mitigate. Information and communication provides management with the ability to record transactions and communicate responsibilities within the organization. Control activities refer to management's safeguarding of assets and segregation of incompatible duties to prevent an individual from both perpetrating a fraud and covering it up in the accounting records. Finally, the monitoring component of internal control requires the company to assess internal control performance over time. The Treadway Commission issued the COSO framework as a comprehensive assessment of internal control effectiveness rather than a single assessment with the purpose of determining whether the entity has the right internal controls over financial reporting.